*Astana

K A Z A K H S T A N

SEA

B E K I S T A N

Khiva

ISSYK-KUL

Almaty
Ile-Alatau
National Park

Bishkek

K Y R G Y Z S T A N

Karakol

T I E N   S H A N

Tashkent

Arslanbob

Samarkand

Osh

Kashgar

Penjikent

C H I N A

Bukhara

T A J I K I S T A N

Dushanbe

Khorog

A F G H A N I S T A N

P A K I S T A N

Samarkand

RECIPES & STORIES FROM CENTRAL ASIA & THE CAUCASUS

Caroline Eden is a contributor to the travel pages of *The Guardian*, *Financial Times*, and *The Telegraph* and has a weekly page in the London *Metro*. She has also reported on Central Asia and the Caucasus for BBC Radio 4. Eleanor Ford has been a recipe developer and editor for the Good Food Channel and *BBC Good Food Magazine*. She has judged The Guild of Food Writers' Awards, was local editor for Zagat's Hong Kong guide, and has been a *Time Out* restaurant reviewer.

Samarkand

RECIPES & STORIES FROM CENTRAL ASIA & THE CAUCASUS

Caroline Eden & Eleanor Ford

food photography Laura Edwards

Kyle Books

"For my mother, Kirsty, an inspiration in and out of the kitchen." Eleanor

"To the memory of my mother who is with me on every journey." Caroline

Published in 2016 by Kyle Books
www.kylebooks.com

Distributed by National Book Network
4501 Forbes Blvd, Suite 200
Lanham, MD 20706
Phone: (800) 462-6420
Fax: (800) 338-4550
customercare@nbnbooks.com

10 9 8 7 6 5 4 3 2 1

ISBN 978 1 909487 42 0

Designer: Patrick Budge
Photographer: Laura Edwards
Food Stylist: Linda Tubby
Props Stylist: Tabitha Hawkins
Project Editor: Sophie Allen
Editorial Assistant: Hannah Coughlin
Americanizer: Christy Lusiak
Production: Nic Jones, Gemma John, and Lisa Pinnell

Library of Congress Control Number: 2016933420

Color reproduction by ALTA London
Printed and bound in China by C&C Offset Printing Co., Ltd.

* All photography by Laura Edwards except see page 224

Contents

Samarkand—a culinary journey through Central Asia

"In all other parts of the world light descends upon earth. From holy Samarkand and Bukhara, it ascends." Local saying

Samarkand—the turquoise city

For centuries, the fabled city Samarkand has been a magnet for merchants, travelers, and conquerors. Its name resonates like those of only a handful of other ancient cities, perhaps Babylon, Rome, or Jerusalem. Say it out loud and it rolls off the tongue: Samarkand. It is seductive.

Set in the valley of the Zerafshan River in Uzbekistan, this turquoise oasis still beguiles modern-day visitors following in the footsteps of Alexander the Great and the mighty Tamerlane. Reflecting its past as a cultural crossroads, this Silk Road stopover has buildings, gardens, fountains, and other cultural treasures whose extraordinary beauty and achievement inspired Islamic architecture across the entire region—from the Mediterranean to India. Sky-blue mosques and sand-colored minarets, fluted domes, madrasas, and monumental mausoleums, their ceramic-tiled and mosaic surfaces dazzling with floral motifs and geometric patterns—the effect is as dizzying and utterly compelling as a mirage in the desert.

For hundreds of years the journey to Samarkand necessitated a Herculean effort. Arduous expeditions, carrying goods between far-off cities like Xi'an and Shiraz, made the trek on two-humped Bactrian camels over endless steppe, through inhospitable mountains, and across shifting sands like the Taklamakan Desert, a parched expanse roughly the size of Italy.

Why? What made men endure scorching heat, numbing cold, and howling winds, losing their minds—and lives—in a bid to reach Samarkand, hidden behind a barricade of mountain, grasslands, and sand? The answer is trade, because from the sixth to the thirteenth centuries, Samarkand experienced an age of unmatched prosperity. It became Asia's great store window, one of the world's finest marketplaces, where everything from rare spices to yak-tail fly whisks were bartered and sold.

Throughout the centuries, the wealth of Samarkand has been legendary. Merchants sought bags of rice and carrots from the Himalayas, cuts of sugar cane, bundles of lemons, plaits of garlic, and sacks of soy beans from eastern Asia. Exchange on the Silk Road traveled in both directions too. From the west toward China went cucumbers, colored glass, and wine grapes. Historian Edward H. Schafer, in his

Top: The Registan, Samarkand; bottom: Interior view of the Shadi Mulk Aka Mausoleum, taken as an Uzbek woman in traditional dress leaves after praying

gorgeously titled book *The Golden Peaches of Samarkand*, describes how "fancy yellow peaches, large as goose eggs were formally gifted to China's Tang empire in the seventh century, symbolizing all the exotic things longed for."

Traders found safety in Samarkand in the form of shelter, dealers, and brokers. Mercenaries too could be hired for the onward journey to fend off slave raiders and bandits. Long after the merchants had departed, their goods and traditions stayed on in this oasis. Sogdian—the language of Samarkand's middlemen—became the language of the commercial world. "Melting pot" is a somewhat exhausted metaphor but it describes Samarkand perfectly. This is a city that has been at the crossroads of food culture for centuries.

Modern-day Samarkand is no longer the mythical place it once was, but the journey to this incredible city is always an exciting one.

The inextricable link between food and travel

It was on such a journey that I decided to write this book. The idea was to bring together the cuisines of seven ethnic groups who had left their mark on Samarkand over the centuries—the Tajiks, Russians, Turks, Jews, Koreans, Caucasians, and the Uzbeks themselves.

Tajiks have lived in Samarkand and Bukhara for centuries and large numbers still do. In mountainous Tajikistan itself, bordered by Kyrgyzstan to the north, Uzbekistan to the northwest, Afghanistan to the south, and China to the east, their cuisine displays a mix of Russian, Uzbek, and perfumed rice dishes, reflecting Persian roots.

A sizeable population of ethnic Russians continues to live in post-Soviet Central Asia. Smoke and brine—traditionally used to preserve food in Russia—infuse the air in homes and restaurants. Sweet earthy borsht and piroshky (fried buns stuffed with potatoes and meat) are ever-present in markets and cafés. Another holdover from the Soviet era is a passion for vodka. Despite their Islamic heritage, many Central Asians enjoy a drink and any new visitor will quickly learn that local hospitality combined with the firepower of a few shots can pack a mean punch (and hangover).

Turks have traded and lived in the region for centuries and Turkish cuisine is imitated and admired across Central Asia. The seventeenth-century Ottoman traveler and diarist Evliya Çelebi described dishes that were prepared for Ottoman Pashas, which chime with the cuisine of Central Asia today: "saffron, çilav (boiled rice), roasted meats, mulberry... meatballs, pistachios, almonds, raisin pilafs of partridge, pomegranate, and soups." Nowadays, popular Turkish restaurants in the Central Asian region tend to serve pides—similar to pizza—mutton casseroles, spitted and grilled lamb, while kebab varieties run into the dozens.

Top: A valley leading up to Song Kol, Kyrgyzstan; Bottom: A market in Samarkand

There are Jews living in Bukhara and Samarkand who claim to be direct descendants of the ten lost tribes of Israel, although historians suggest it is more likely that they arrived at the behest of the fearsome tribal leader, Tamerlane. As he blazed a trail through Asia in the fourteenth century, he brought Jewish dyers and weavers from the Middle East back to his splendid blue-tiled city of Samarkand. Over time, oppressive leadership and the collapse of the Soviet Union meant that these Jews became one of the most detached Jewish communities in the world. Through it all, many culinary traditions were guarded and preserved, even though today, only around a thousand Jews remain in Uzbekistan. Uzbek Jewish cuisine is a comingling of Persia's vegetable-studded pilafs and Russia's heavy meat dishes. It is characterized by light spices—a little cumin, coriander, turmeric, pepper, and chile—and delicate flavors intensified by herbs, onion, and garlic.

The peoples of Central Asia have never developed a taste for fiery food but one exception is the Korean diaspora, known as the *Koryo-Saram*. Stalin deported half a million Koreans to Central Asia during the Second World War, many of whom stayed on and have become the purveyors of pepped-up flavors. Dishes like pickled cucumber and beef ribbons give more than a nod to chile, and cabbage-heavy kimchi—Korea's national dish—is increasingly popular in Central Asian capitals. It's also the case that no matter how remote the market in Uzbekistan, you will always find a Korean woman selling take-out bags of carrot salad.

The Caucasians—Georgians, Azeris, and Armenians—are all historically connected to Central Asia. During the Persian Empire, fierce Armenian warriors left their homelands to travel the Silk Road, fighting beside local warlords in exchange for trading rights. Clergy from the Caucasus also left their monasteries to join far-flung theological debates. During the fourteenth century, a group of Armenian clergy traveled as far as the Chinese border to build a monastery named after Saint Matthew. They took their culinary traditions with them and many cultural interchanges resulted. Small communities of Armenians reside in all the nations of Central Asia.

This book is a celebration of the richness and diversity of this remarkable Asian heartland and the culinary heritage of its distinct populations. It is the combined work of two friends, both travelers and writers, bonded by a passion for good food and adventures into countries very different from home. The voice you'll hear in the travel and food essays is mine while that in the recipes is Eleanor's.

Previous page: Top left: "Stolovaya"—canteen in the middle of nowhere along the Pamir highway south of Murghab, Tajikistan; Top right: Pickles for sale in Baku, Azerbaijan; Bottom left: Watermelons for sale, Azerbaijan; Bottom middle: Mural and Ladas in Nukus, Karakalpakstan, Uzbekistan; Bottom right: Shepherds living in yurts in the mountain pasture of Song Kol, Kyrgyzstan; This page: A market in Samarkand

Dazzling bazaars, golden bread, and a blanket of stars

When I first arrived in Samarkand in 2009, weary from exploring the Pamir Mountains, its atmosphere shook me. The skyline is filled with monolithic Soviet blocks, colossal sky-blue domed mosques, and pale desert-hued minarets. At street level, tangled bazaars overflowed, cauldrons of plov bubbled on the side of the

road, and butchers hacked away at sides of beef on tree stumps used as cutting boards. Melons the size of a horse's head were crammed into the boots of Lada cars, store fronts were festooned with dizzying bolts of ikat and suzani fabric bearing pomegranate motifs, while legions of babushki (elderly ladies) pushed vintage prams that carried not mewling babies but golden discs of bread. It's like time travel, I said, echoing the words of countless travelers before me.

At daybreak, before the arrival of pilgrims, I had wandered alone in the otherworldly necropolis of the Shah-i-Zinda as imams chanted. That night, I ate tandoor-fresh bread and sliced crescents of juicy melon with a jewel handled knife beneath a blanket of stars. Can any other place on earth provide such a feast for the senses?

My first encounter with Samarkand not only provided a romantic passage back to the fourteenth century and Tamerlane's capital (see page 31)—it also sowed the seed for this book.

Over the ensuing years I completed a dozen or so trips to Central Asia, Turkey, Russia, and the Caucasus. On these adventures I dined in mountain villages, in city centers, by glittering lakes, and out on the steppe. I ate borscht while playing backgammon with war veterans in Soviet-style canteens, slurped gently seasoned laghman (noodles) in yurt cafés, and enjoyed unending hospitality in people's homes. By avoiding the "tourist" restaurants it is easy to eat well in the former Soviet Union; hospitality is a cult in all these countries. It oils the wheels and it is justifiably legendary. In Samarkand you can expect a genuine welcome, for "the guest is the first person in the home."

I fast discovered an enormous diversity of food cultures, from Russian-style borscht to Turkish-style shashlik, and dishes that at first seemed familiar but were not—like the omnipresent plov, which is similar to a Persian pilaf, and samsa, which is like an Indian samosa. Everywhere I went I feasted on fruit fit for kings—all of it always criminally cheap. The aromatic apricots in the Pamir Mountains of Tajikistan, the famous golden peaches of Uzbekistan, and the bullet-shaped grapes in Kyrgyzstan, made me realize what we in the West have lost in flavor in the name of convenience. Most of all, I discovered that this food culture that straddles many borders is a bit like matryoshka, those brilliantly kitsch Russian dolls. As soon as you unveil one, another presents itself. And at the heart of it all was Samarkand, which has sat at the crossroads of food culture for centuries. As a mere city its location is narrow, but its scope is extraordinarily wide.

CAROLINE EDEN

Previous pages: The Registan, Samarkand, with its famously multicoloured tiles; This page top: Siyob Bazaar, Samarkand; Bottom: Turgen Valley, Almaty District, Kazakhstan

The ingredients, flavors, and recipes

Although we cover a vast region in this book, there are common threads running through all the different cuisines. Being largely landlocked, meat makes up a huge part of the diet: that can mean beef, lamb, goat, camel, horse, and chicken. Kebabs and shashliks are mainstays from Turkey to Afghanistan. Every country has its own wonderful versions of pilafs or plovs as well as flatbreads, including the ubiquitous non. Central Asians are justly proud of their dairy produce and eat, drink, dry, and ferment milk in many different ways. Yogurt, in various forms, will be found on most tables, along with smetana (sour cream) and suzma (yogurt cheese).

The flavors of Central Asian cooking reflect its position, where very different culinary worlds meet. Spices are key, as you would expect from countries crossed by the Silk Road, yet they are used judiciously, to enhance flavors of the main ingredients rather than mask them. Any heat in Central Asian food tends to come from whole peppers and Turkish red or Aleppo pepper and black pepper; dried chile is used more sparingly still. Uzbek cumin is punchier than the seeds we buy at home and is frequently—if cautiously—used as is warm-scented cinnamon and the tart, lemon flavor of ground sumac berries introduces an Iranian note. Herbs, however, are used in abundance—tarragon and basil lend European accents, cilantro adds an Eastern element and dill, of course, so much a flavor of Russian cooking, punctuates many dishes.

Fruits, both fresh and dried, feature widely. Throughout this book you'll see the returning stars of pomegranates, apples, apricots, raisins, and sour cherries. Tartness often comes from barberries, a fall fruit. Salads are seasoned with wine vinegar along with handfuls of fresh herbs and, sometimes, pomegranate seeds. Sheep fat and cottonseed oil are traditionally used much more than vegetable and olive oils. Nuts too—walnuts, pistachios, and hazelnuts—are not only snacks, but ground into rich sauces, folded into rice, or scattered over pastry dough. Then there is rosewater and petals—popular in both Armenian cooking and poetry.

Most of the ingredients should be familiar and easily available; a few may require a trip to a Turkish or Middle Eastern store. (You can see a crossover of food culture with Iran, and many of the more unusual ingredients such as pomegranate molasses, barberries, and lavash bread are common to Persian, Caucasian, and Turkic cuisines.)

In writing *Samarkand* we set out to provide a tasting of the regional cuisine with a collection of recipes from Central Asia and beyond, that will prove inspiring and accessible to the home cook. Some of these recipes are authentic renditions of

Right: Spices at Almaty market, Kazakhstan; Overleaf: Top left: Winter time in Panfilov park, a trailer selling beer, pop, and snacks in Almaty; Top right: Roof of a tea house in Bukhara, Uzbekistan; Bottom left: Uzbeks on pilgramage to the Registan, Samarkand; Bottom middle: Pamir Highway; Bottom right: Bustling crowd in Bukhara

dishes from the road, exactly as Caroline and I have eaten them on our travels, while others are simplified or playful, using traditional pairings of ingredients. A few recipes are inspired by neighboring Afghanistan as well as Xinjiang in northwest China (home to the Muslim Turkic Uighurs). All are connected through the legacy of the former Soviet Union and trade routes of the Silk Road.

Our hope is that these recipes and culinary tales will introduce you to new flavors and fresh ideas and inspire interest in an unfamiliar part of the world and its extraordinary food heritage.

ELEANOR FORD

A Shared Table

Tomatoes, Dill, and Purple Basil

Serves 2 to 4

½ small onion
1 teaspoon sugar
pinch of sea salt
pinch of dried chile flakes
1¼ pounds sweet, ripe tomatoes
1 tablespoon chopped dill
  fronds
1 tablespoon shredded
  purple basil
½ tablespoon finely chopped
  cilantro leaves

Known endearingly to Uzbeks as "sweetie hottie," this salad makes the best of sweet and juicy tomatoes, with chile flakes lending the hot. Another version adds cucumber and the dish becomes known as "sugar water," as the cucumber takes on all the sweetness of the tomatoes. Using three distinctly flavored herbs adds another layer of interest.

Slice the onion into half moons as paper-thin as possible and put in a bowl of cold salted water for 10 minutes (this removes some of the astringency). Drain.

Mix together the sugar, salt, and chile flakes.

Slice the tomatoes and start layering on a serving platter, scattering with the onion, herbs, and sweet chile salt as you go. Serve at room temperature.

Walnut-stuffed Eggplant Rolls

Serves 4

2 medium eggplants

For the stuffing
2 cups shelled walnuts
seeds of ½ pomegranate
1 tablespoon chopped
   cilantro leaves
1 small garlic clove, crushed
1 green chile, seeded,
   finely sliced
2 tablespoons olive oil,
   plus extra for brushing
juice of 1 lemon
sea salt and freshly ground
   black pepper

pomegranate molasses,
   to serve

All over the Caucasus, people traditionally stuff eggplants with walnuts and pomegranate seeds to be pickled and preserved for the long winter months. This is a fresh version of the Georgian dish *badrijani nigvzit*, using grilled eggplants instead, but with the same flavors. Try to use narrow eggplants, rather than bulbous ones, to give you long slices for rolling.

Preheat the oven to 350°F. Spread the walnuts out on a baking sheet and toast in the oven for 5 to 10 minutes until golden. Pour them onto a clean kitchen towel and rub off and discard the skins. Let cool.

Make the stuffing by pounding the walnuts into a rubble using a mortar and pestle. Stir in the pomegranate seeds, cilantro, garlic, and chile. Slacken the mixture with 2 tablespoons of olive oil, the lemon juice, and season with salt. Set aside for the flavors to meld.

Preheat a ridged grill pan until really hot. Remove the stem from the eggplants and carefully cut each lengthwise into slices less than ½-inch thick. Discard the skin side slices. Brush each slice generously with olive oil on both sides and season. Lay a few slices on the hot pan and cook until completely soft and charred on both sides. Set aside while you cook the remaining batches.

Spread the eggplant slices with the walnut stuffing and roll into cylinders. You can use cocktail sticks to keep the rolls together. Serve at room temperature drizzled with pomegranate molasses.

Cucumbers with Yogurt and Mulberries

Serves 2 to 4

4 Persian or 1½ English
  cucumbers, peeled, halved
  lengthwise, and seeded
  using a teaspoon
sea salt and freshly ground
  black pepper
½ cup plain yogurt
1 tablespoon tarragon leaves
1 tablespoon mint leaves, torn
a handful of fresh mulberries
  or 1 tablespoon dried sour
  cherries or dried mulberries

pomegranate molasses,
  to serve

The forests of Central Asia are filled with wild nut and fruit trees, including walnuts, pistachios, almonds, apples, plums, cherries, and mulberries. When mulberries come into season, throngs of customers from Turkey to Uzbekistan line up at market stalls, eager to buy the clustered fruits and for preserving to get underway to ensure a supply during the long winter months.

This is a take on the Persian cucumber and yogurt salads popular throughout the region. If mulberries aren't in season, dried mulberries work well, lending the fragrance, if not the tang, of the fresh. Sour cherries also make a fitting substitute with their sweet-sharp notes.

Cut the cucumber halves into small, even-sized cubes. Season with salt and pepper, then dress with the yogurt and herbs. Scatter with the mulberries and serve with a slick of sweet-tart pomegranate molasses on top.

Koryo Spicy Carrots

Serves 4

1 pound carrots, peeled
½ teaspoon sea salt
1 teaspoon sesame seeds
1 teaspoon coriander seeds
½ teaspoon cumin seeds
3 tablespoons rice vinegar
    or cider vinegar
2 teaspoons honey
1 garlic clove, crushed
1 to 2 bird's eye chiles, seeded
    and finely chopped
2 tablespoons sunflower oil
a handful of cilantro leaves

Half a million Koreans arrived in Central Asia as deportees during World War II. Today, Uzbekistan has the largest population, but the *Koryo-saram* (literally "Korea persons") can be found selling their spicy pickled salads in bazaars throughout Central Asia. Without the right cabbage to make kimchi, Korea's signature dish, they developed new salads that, until recently, weren't known in Korea itself. This carrot version, representing a real fusion of Central and Eastern Asian cooking, is the most popular. Heat and tang from the East are paired with the earthiness of cumin and coriander, redolent of the local spice markets.

Shred the carrots into long, thin strands. A food processor or spiralizer is best for this, but you could use a grater or mandolin, or julienne with a sharp knife. Toss with the salt and set aside for 1 hour to soften.

Toast the sesame, coriander, and cumin seeds in a dry pan until fragrant. Pour into a mortar and lightly crush, just to crack the coriander seeds. Whisk in the vinegar, honey, garlic, and chiles. Finally, whisk in the oil and taste the dressing to decide whether to adjust the sweet-sour balance.

Dress the carrots. The dish is best left for a few hours to pickle slightly. Scatter with the fresh cilantro before serving.

Samarkand—Tamerlane's center of the universe

In 1370 Tamerlane, "Conqueror of the World," achieved supremacy by defeating khanates and Ottoman sultans, and by gaining control of trade routes from India to Syria. Born just south of Samarkand, Tamerlane was a nomad with a thirst for blood (his men beheaded 10,000 Hindus in an hour while plundering Delhi) and women (he had 12 wives). At its height, his empire stretched from the Indus Valley to the Black Sea and under his rule Samarkand became a mythical city and, once again, an intellectual and religious center. From the lands he conquered—Asia Minor, Persia, and India—he returned with the finest masons, painters, weavers, silversmiths, and tile-glazers to beautify his beloved Samarkand. In the early fifteenth century, Castilian envoy Ruy Gonzalez de Clavijo, noted in his book *Embassy to Tamerlane* that the markets of Samarkand had rare leathers and linens from Russia and Tartary, while from Cathay came "silk stuffs that are the finest in the world." He went on: "Thence too is brought musk, balas rubies, and diamonds, also pearls, lastly rhubarb. From India there are brought spices which are the most costly of the kind, such as nutmegs, cloves, cinnamon, and ginger."

Despite his fearsome reputation, Tamerlane enjoyed nothing more than playing chess (he invented his own version with twice the number of pieces on the board), drinking, and feasting. De Clavijo described an exceptionally meaty royal feast that consisted of "a quantity of mutton, roast, boiled, and in stews, also horse-meat roasted... knots of the horse-tripe in balls of the size of a fist, with a sheep's head all of a piece." Food was cheap and the needs of the people of Samarkand were satisfied under Tamerlane's reign. He was a spectacular host, throwing lavish parties in ornate tents decorated with plundered treasures, and ordered fountains, gardens, and caravanserai to be laid out, as well as the marketplace in front of Samarkand's iconic Registan to which modern-day traders and tourists still flock. Tamerlane is buried in Samarkand's mausoleum, Gur-e-Amir, along with his two sons and grandsons, his chamber decorated with ornate vaulted niches and paintings.

Radish, Cucumber, and Herbs

Serves 6

10½ ounces cucumber (about 1 large), halved lengthwise and seeded
14 ounces red radishes (about 3½ cups chopped)
¾ cup scallions, finely sliced
3 cups cilantro leaves, finely chopped
¼ cup plus 2 tablespoons dill fronds, finely chopped
1 teaspoon sugar
½ teaspoon dried chile flakes
sea salt and freshly ground black pepper

This recipe is for the sort of salad you will find on tables across Uzbekistan. It is fresh, peppery, and refreshing, perfect for pairing with mutton or lamb.

Splashes of pink and emerald from the radish and cucumber skins in among the pastel hues give the salad a bright appearance as well as a refreshing flavor to offset a meat-heavy meal. It is surprisingly good, given the ease with which it can be thrown together.

Cut the cucumber halves and radishes into small, even-sized cubes. Toss with the scallions, herbs, sugar and dried chile flakes, then then season well with salt and pepper. Serve at once.

Grated Zucchini with Pine Nuts and Poppy Seeds

Serves 4

4 small or 2 large zucchini, unpeeled
1 tablespoon poppy seeds
2 tablespoons pine nuts, lightly toasted
2 teaspoons dried rose petals
zest and juice of ½ lemon
2 tablespoons olive oil
1 teaspoon sugar
½ teaspoon ground sumac
a handful of cilantro leaves
sea salt and freshly ground black pepper

Raw zucchini has a pleasing crunch and nutty flavor that pairs well with the sweet taste of poppy seeds and pine nuts. In summer, a mix of green and yellow zucchini looks lovely with the pink rose petals.

Coarsely grate the zucchini into a bowl using a box grater.

Toss with the remaining ingredients and season with salt and pepper. An extra pinch of salt flakes over the top is good as well.

Serve immediately (it will soon get watery).

Green Olive and Walnut Salad

Serves 2 to 4

¾ cup shelled walnuts
1 teaspoon cumin seeds
¾ cup green olives, pitted
1 red chile, seeded and
  finely chopped
1 garlic clove, crushed
1 tablespoon dill fronds,
  chopped
1 tablespoon thyme leaves
1 tablespoon extra virgin
  olive oil
1 tablespoon walnut oil
juice of ½ lemon
sea salt and freshly ground
  black pepper
warm flatbread, to serve

Half salad, half salsa, and totally delicious. I first ate this in Istanbul and was blown away by the combination of flavors from East and West. The Mediterranean olives and thyme pair so well with two Central Asian stalwarts, cumin and dill. Make sure you use really good green olives.

Preheat the oven to 350°F. Spread the walnuts out on a baking sheet and toast in the oven for 5 to 10 minutes until golden. Transfer them onto a clean kitchen towel and rub off and discard the skins. Chop the nuts.

Toast the cumin seeds in a dry pan until fragrant.

Coarsely chop the olives. Combine them with all the other ingredients and leave for 10 minutes for the flavors to meld. Taste and adjust the seasoning, if needed. Serve with flatbread.

Mushroom Caviar

Serves 2 to 4

3 tablespoons butter
9 ounces chestnut mushrooms,
  finely chopped (about
  3½ cups)
2 large shallots, finely chopped
2 garlic cloves, crushed
½ teaspoon paprika
½ teaspoon cayenne
2 tablespoons sour cream
2 tablespoons toasted pine nuts
1 tablespoon finely chopped
  flat-leaf parsley leaves
good squeeze of lemon juice
sea salt and freshly ground
  black pepper
baby blinis, to serve

Russians love mushrooms, which they view as gifts of the forest. Mushroom caviar—aka poor man's caviar—is a silky, rich pâté that makes the most of the earthy, nutty flavor of the mushrooms. It is ideal served on baby blinis as *zakuski* (small bites). A food processor makes light work of the chopping.

Melt the butter in a large frying pan over high heat. When it is foaming, add the mushrooms and shallots. Cook for 5 minutes to cook off the liquid they give out, stirring frequently. Add the garlic and cook for another minute before removing the pan from the heat.

Stir through the remaining ingredients and season generously with lemon juice, salt, and pepper. Serve slightly warm or at room temperature with buckwheat blinis or good bread.

Salt-massaged Cabbage

Serves 4

½ pointed cabbage, core
  removed and coarsely
  shredded
1 carrot, finely shredded
1 large red chile, seeded
  and thickly sliced
1 teaspoon sea salt
1 teaspoon sugar
a large handful of beansprouts
2 tablespoons rice vinegar or
  cider vinegar
1 tablespoon chopped
  cilantro leaves
1 tablespoon chopped
  dill fronds

This salad is completely raw, with all the fresh flavor to go with it. However, massaging the vegetables with salt and sugar, as they do in Kazakhstan, softens and breaks down their tough fibers in a similar way to cooking or pickling the vegetables, leaving just a little pleasing crunch.

Combine the cabbage, carrot, and chile in a large bowl. Sprinkle with the salt and sugar, and use your hands to massage the ingredients togther for about 5 minutes.

Mix in the beansprouts and set aside for 15 minutes, during which time the juices will puddle in the bottom of the bowl. Discard the juices, rinse the vegetables under cold running water, and drain well.

Before serving, dress with the vinegar and fresh herbs.

Four Caucasian Dips

Across the region readily available fruit, vegetables, nuts, and leaves are turned into tasty dips to serve as appetizers. Georgia's specialty, pkhali, is traditionally made using a variety of chopped green leaves including spinach, nettles, and beet greens.

Georgian Spinach Pkhali

14 ounces spinach, washed and
  thick stems removed
¾ cup shelled walnuts
3 scallions, chopped
1 garlic clove, crushed
a small bunch of cilantro
  leaves
a handful of tarragon leaves
½ teaspoon paprika
¼ teaspoon ground fenugreek
  (optional)
2 tablespoons olive oil
1 tablespoon white wine
  vinegar
sea salt and freshly ground
  black pepper
seeds of ½ pomegranate,
  to garnish

Bring a large pan of water to a boil, add the spinach, and cook until just wilted. Drain and put into iced water to cool. Drain once more and squeeze well to remove as much liquid as possible. Chop the spinach finely, by hand rather than in the food processor, to preserve some texture.

Put the remaining ingredients, except the pomegranate, in a food processor. Blend to a purée, then stir through the spinach. Taste for seasoning.

Serve the green pkhali scattered with a ruby-red shower of pomegranate seeds.

Beets, Prune, and Mint

3 medium raw beets, unpeeled
3 prunes, pitted
1 tablespoon mint leaves
2 garlic cloves, crushed
2 tablespoons lemon juice
1 tablespoon vodka
sea salt
½ cup chopped walnuts, toasted
2 tablespoons sour cream

Preheat the oven to 400°F.

Wrap the whole beets individually in aluminum foil and roast for 45 minutes to 1 hour, until a skewer easily pierces the flesh. Cool then peel.

Put the beets in a food processor with the prunes, mint, garlic, lemon juice, and vodka. Season with salt and purée until smooth. Transfer to a serving bowl, stir in the walnuts, then swirl through the sour cream, making ripples in the pink purée. Serve at room temperature.

Smoky Eggplant Caviar

1 large eggplant
1 garlic clove, crushed
½ teaspoon Turkish red pepper or Aleppo pepper
2 tablespoons olive oil
1 tablespoon lemon juice
seeds of ½ pomegranate
a handful of mint, cilantro leaves, or basil leaves, chopped
sea salt

If you have a gas burner, set the eggplant directly over the open flame and let cook, turning occasionally with tongs, until the skin is blackened and the flesh is completely soft. Alternatively, halve the eggplant lengthwise and cook skin-side up under a hot broiler until tender and collapsed.

Discard the charred skin and drain off any liquid.

Mash the smoky eggplant flesh with a fork and stir through the remaining ingredients. Season with salt and serve at room temperature.

Azeri Apple and Walnut

2 sweet apples, peeled, cored, and coarsely chopped
½ cup shelled walnuts
2 tablespoons verjuice (unripe grape juice) or lemon juice

Put the apples in a small pan with 1 tablespoon of water. Cover and set over medium heat for about 15 minutes until tender. Let cool.

Transfer the apple and any juices from the pan to a food processor with the walnuts and verjuice. Blend to a coarse purée.

Suzma

2½ cups full-fat Greek yogurt
sea salt

Central Asia has vast flat plains, including the world's largest steppe region, "the Great Steppe," as well as mountain regions. This expanse of grassland is renowned for its rich, smooth dairy products made from cow, goat, sheep, horse, and even camel milk. Suzma is a tangy yogurt cheese that is spooned into soups, mixed into salads, or eaten with bread and fresh tomatoes as a simple meal.

You can make your own yogurt-based suzma, as in this recipe, or substitute the yogurt for cottage or cream cheese, sharpened with a squeeze of lemon juice.

Start a day or two before you want to serve. Season the yogurt with a generous pinch of salt. Hang a muslin or cheesecloth bag over a bowl, or line a colander with two pieces of paper towel and set it in a shallow dish. Pour in the yogurt and tie the muslin at the top to form a tight bundle (or cover the colander with plastic wrap) and leave in a cool place for 24 to 36 hours for the liquid to drain off and the yogurt to thicken. Discard the liquid.

You can either eat the suzma as it is, or flavor it in one of the ways below.

Green Suzma
Finely chop the white and green parts of 4 scallions, and a small bunch each of cilantro, dill, and parsley. Stir through the suzma and season with salt and pepper.

White Suzma
Stir in 1 crushed garlic clove and 1 teaspoon of finely chopped dill. Season with salt and pepper.

Pink Suzma
Blend 2 cooked beets until smooth. Stir into the suzma with 1 teaspoon of sugar. Season with salt and pepper.

Tajik Bread Salad

Serves 2 to 4
as an appetizer or light lunch

For the dressing

2 tablespoons lemon juice

1 tablespoon rice vinegar or
  cider vinegar

1 teaspoon sugar

¾ teaspoon ground
  coriander

5 tablespoons extra virgin
  olive oil

sea salt

For the salad

2 pita breads

2 tablespoons extra virgin
  olive oil

4 large ripe tomatoes, chopped

½ cucumber, halved
  lengthwise, seeded using a
  spoon, and sliced

3 scallions, thinly sliced

a small bunch of cilantro,
  leaves chopped

a small bunch of dill fronds,
  chopped

½ cup feta cheese

non bread (see page 152),
  to serve

Crisp shards of flatbread give crunch to this dish, which lies somewhere between a Greek salad and Levantine *fattoush*. Typically, it is served in Tajikistan on a large communal wooden platter along with hot, flaky, non bread for everyone to scoop up the salty cheese and fresh vegetables. More authentically, Tajiks make a cheese from yogurt simmered with salt until thickened to warm curds, but feta makes a good substitute.

For the dressing, mix the lemon juice, vinegar, sugar, and ground coriander in a bowl. Gradually whisk in the olive oil until well blended and season with salt.

For the salad, preheat the oven to 375°F.

Split and open the pita breads into four halves and cut these into thin triangles. Brush with the olive oil. Toast in the oven for about 10 minutes until golden. They will crisp as they cool.

Put the tomatoes, cucumber, and scallions in a large serving dish, and mix with the dressing and herbs. Crumble over the feta, then add the pita shards. Toss once and serve immediately with hot non.

Lunch on the road to Samarkand

It is 6am and the sun is bleaching the mountains around the Tajik capital Dushanbe. The driver of our shared taxi heading west, finally satisfied that every seat in his Mitsubishi Pajero is full, lights another cigarette and noses out of the capital. For the next undisclosed number of hours ("maybe eight, maybe 12," I am told) we will bounce our way through the remote and desolate Fan Mountains to Penjikent, a place of windswept ancient ruins, which will serve as our fifth-century pitstop.

Penjikent, known as the Pompeii of Central Asia, is a ruined ancient city where remarkable frescoes were excavated. From here, a two-hour journey—and iffy border crossing—will take me into Uzbekistan and finally, to the city of Samarkand. The anticipation rises. My mind fills with images of turquoise tile-work, towering madrassas and Tamerlane's marauding horsemen.

We travel not for trafficking alone;
By hotter winds our fiery hearts are fanned:
For lust of knowing what should not be known,
We make the Golden Road to Samarkand.

Throughout its long history Samarkand has inspired poets to write, and these famous lines by James Elroy Flecker are on my mind as the journey begins. So too is breakfast. A quick rummage in my bag tells me that once again the romance of the road has got in the way of sense and I realize, stomach rumbling, that I haven't packed a ration of survival food. As our car kicks up dust on hairpin bends, nothing we pass is edible. Spotting our car, women wearing psychedelic paisley-print headscarves offer us the nomadic snack of qurut. I decline glumly, for these brackish dried yogurt balls are dehydrating salt bombs that make a decent partner for beer, but are not much good for breakfast. Rivers curl between deep valleys and peaks rise higher than the Alps. It is a nettlesome but spectacular journey.

Three hours in and my eyes sting with tiredness. Sleep had not come easily at the Hotel Vakhsh in Dushanbe where I had spent two days waiting for my Uzbek visa. Once occupied by mujahideen rebels, today it is a Soviet-style hotel where you deposit your jewelry to reserve a room and sleep under itchy sheets. Grim-faced "floor ladies," their hair dyed cherry-red, keep a watchful eye on those coming and going, mainly drunk businessmen. I had been glad to leave.

Ravenous now, we roll into Penjikent at dusk. A pink glow hovers over the ruins that mark a former major city on the Silk Road. Only grass-tufted foundations are visible today, but once a palace stood here with columns in the shape of dancing girls.

My fixer in Dushanbe had hooked me up with Firdauz, a local man who runs a homestay. As promised, he is there to meet me and leads the way to his low-slung house set around a courtyard and small orchard. As I finish unpacking a few essentials, Firdauz motions me into their dining room. There is little furniture. Red and orange Bukharan rugs cover both floors and walls. In the corner, video footage is showing a Tajik wedding. Two Spanish travelers sit, watching the film. What my hungry eyes fix on in the scenes of celebration is a bubbling *kazan* of plov, big enough to feed several hundred.

Then, in comes Firdauz's wife, Fatima. Cue shakarob! Cue shurbo! Cue vodka! The shakarob—a simple salad of flaky fatir flatbread, tomatoes, onion, and yogurt—has all the thirst-quenching benefits of an energy drink. I hoover it up in tandem with the steaming shurbo, a potato broth laced with herbs, as plates of sizzling shashlik are ferried out from the kitchen. I laugh and exchange travel tales with my hosts and the two Spaniards. We toast everything from "friendship" to "Samarkand." The vodka and conversation flow. Worn out and sated at long last, I almost wept.

Note: Sadly the Penjikent-Samarkand border crossing is currently closed to foreigners. Border crossings in Central Asia change like the wind, so always check before you set out. The best website with up-to-date information is caravanistan.com

Selling qurut on the roadside in Uzbekistan

Turkish Spoon Salad

Serves 6

6 juicy plum tomatoes
1 red bell pepper
1 cucumber, peeled and halved
  lengthwise
2 red chiles, seeded and
  finely chopped
1 shallot, finely chopped
2 tablespoons olive oil
1 tablespoon red wine vinegar
2 tablespoons pomegranate
  molasses
2 teaspoons harissa
seeds of ½ pomegranate
3 tablespoons finely chopped
  flat-leaf parsley leaves
2 tablespoons finely chopped
  mint
sea salt and freshly ground
  black pepper
sugar (optional)

The name of this salad refers to its spoonable consistency. Serve as part of a mezze platter or as a salsa.

Cut a cross in the base of each tomato and plunge into boiling water for 30 seconds. Refresh in cold water before peeling.

Scorch the whole red bell pepper over an open flame or under a hot broiler, then rub off the blackened skin.

Remove the seeds from the tomatoes, bell pepper, and cucumber, and chop them all into very small dice. Transfer to a bowl, add the chiles and shallot, and tumble the vegetables together. Dress with the olive oil, vinegar, pomegranate molasses, and harissa. Season with salt and pepper and set aside for 30 minutes for the flavors to meld.

Stir through the pomegranate seeds and herbs. Taste before serving—the spoon salad should be fresh, spicy, and tart. You may need to balance the flavors with a little more salt or vinegar, or a pinch of sugar.

Spicy Meat Dolma

Makes 12

7 ounces ground beef

1 shallot, finely chopped

1 red chile, seeded and
finely chopped

1 tablespoon barberries
or dried unsweetened
cranberries

½ teaspoon paprika

¼ teaspoon cayenne pepper

¼ teaspoon ground cumin

2 tablespoons finely chopped
flat-leaf parsley leaves

sea salt and freshly ground
black pepper

16 vine leaves, in brine
or fresh

2 tablespoons olive oil

1 onion, sliced

1 carrot, sliced

4 tomatoes, diced

Greek yogurt, to serve

Stuffed vine leaves are popular from Central Asia through to Turkey, the Mediterranean, and Eastern Europe. Typically, the filling is a mixture of meat and rice, while other fillers for the parcels can be made using cabbage leaves or even hollowed vegetables. In Tashkent I tried a sophisticated version where vine leaf parcels were filled with spiced meat and no rice, making a lighter addition to a shared table rather than a substantial main meal.

Mix the ground beef with the shallot, chile, barberries, spices, and parsley. Season with salt and pepper. Set a small amount of the mixture aside, then use your hands to shape the rest into 12 sausage shapes.

Put the vine leaves in a colander and pour over hot water to rinse off the brine (or blanch fresh leaves in boiling water for 30 seconds to soften). Choose the 12 largest vine leaves and remove the stalks. Lay a leaf on the surface with the stalk end toward you. Sit a sausage on top, roll up the leaf to just cover the filling, then draw in the sides and continue rolling to make a neat parcel. Repeat with the remaining leaves.

Select a casserole pan that will accommodate all 12 dolmas snugly in a single layer. Heat the oil and add the reserved meat mixture—it will help give flavor to the stock. Cook over medium heat until golden, then add the onion and caramelize. Add the carrot and tomatoes, and cook for another minute or two until beginning to soften. Season with salt, then lay the dolmas on top, seam-side down. Add enough hot water to the pan to come three-quarters of the way up the dolmas. Cover with the remaining vine leaves—broken ones unsuitable for stuffing are perfect here—then use a plate a little smaller than the pan to weigh the stuffed leaves down. Bring to a gentle simmer and cook the dolmas for 40 minutes. Let cool in their cooking juice.

Drain and serve at room temperature with Greek yogurt.

Soups

Yogurt, Cucumber, and Rose Petal Soup

Serves 4

4 Persian cucumbers or
  1 English cucumber, coarsely
  chopped
2 cups plain yogurt
2 scallions, chopped
2 tablespoons mint leaves,
  plus extra to serve
2 tablespoons tarragon leaves
2 tablespoons dill fronds
1 garlic clove, crushed
½ teaspoon dried mint
½ teaspoon ground sumac
1 teaspoon rosewater
2 tablespoons dried rose
  petals
sea salt and freshly ground
  black pepper

A refreshing, iced soup for a hot day, and it couldn't be simpler to make. Persian cucumbers, compared with the ones we are more familiar with, are smaller, sweeter, and seedless.

Put all the ingredients in a blender, but reserve half the rose petals and some mint leaves for garnish. Add ¾ cup water and blend until smooth. Add a little more water if you want a thinner consistency. Season with salt and black pepper.

Serve the soup chilled with a few ice cubes dropped in and topped with a scattering of mint and rose petals.

Summer Borscht with Sour Cream and Chives

Serves 4

4 beets, peeled and
  coarsely chopped
3 carrots, coarsely chopped
2 celery stalks, chopped
1 small onion, coarsely
  chopped
1 (14-ounce) can chopped
  tomatoes
1 garlic clove, chopped
1 bay leaf
4 black peppercorns
2 cloves
1 teaspoon sugar
sea salt

To serve
lemon juice
sour cream
snipped chives

This is an elegant version of borscht, a clear, ruby-hued broth served chilled, rather than the heartier beet soups suited to the long winter months. If you have made Rye Bread Kvas (see page 177), try adding a splash to the finished soup.

Put the vegetables and aromatics into a large pan and cover with 5 cups of cold water. Season with the sugar and salt. Bring to a boil, reduce to a simmer, and cook for 40 minutes.

Strain through a fine sieve, reserving the broth and discarding the vegetables (which will have lost their flavor). Let cool, then taste for seasoning. A squeeze of lemon juice will brighten the flavor.

Serve the broth chilled, with a dollop of sour cream and a scattering of chives.

Fruits of the Earth— foraging in the High Pamirs

I have one mission left to complete before leaving the wild and woolly Pamir Mountains in eastern Tajikistan: lunch with Mr. Parpi Shah, aka "King of the Mountain Grass."

Wearing a flat cap and slacks, Shah leads me from the main road in Khorog, the regional capital, up some stairs to his modern Soviet-style apartment. He sits me next to his son, a snow leopard tracker, before vanishing behind a curtain to rummage eagerly in his medicine cabinet. Five minutes later he reappears, herbs in hand, and then disappears with them into the kitchen.

Actor, medicine man, and cook, Shah, who looks considerably younger than his 70 years, thinks nothing of strapping on a backpack and heading up into the foothills of the nearby 24,000-foot peaks of the Pamir Mountains where, depending on the season, he forages for dog rose berries (which he uses to make tea), scented apricots, and some unidentifiable roots known locally as "ibex grass," which are collected as a natural aid for digestion. Here, in the bleak but starkly beautiful *bam-i-dunya* (literally "the roof of the world" in Persian), creative cuisine rules supreme.

Mountains cover 93 percent of the land in the little republic of Tajikistan, which, slightly bigger than Greece, lies wedged in the remote highlands of Central Asia. It has Kyrgyzstan to the north, Uzbekistan to the northwest, China to the east, and Afghanistan to the south, the border of which—little more than a river—runs close to Shah's house. In the 1890s, amid the dry vertical peaks of this moonscape-like terrain, Moscow set up military garrisons during the Great Game when Russia and British India were vying for power in the region.

The Pamiri people are completely different from the Tajiks who live in the lowlands and across the Uzbekistan border in cities like Samarkand. They are Ismailis and their spiritual leader is the Aga Khan, whose framed picture is found in almost every Pamiri household. In these parts, the current Swiss-born Aga Khan is a worldly savior who stepped in and organized emergency food supplies during the dismal years after the collapse of the Soviet Union when, after the sudden termination of aid from Moscow, many Pamiris faced famine. Food is never ever taken for granted in this harsh mountain environment and the huge, curling, ibex-horn roadside shrines, called *oston*, serve as reminders of successful hunting trips that result in celebratory community feasts.

Thirty minutes later, Shah emerges from his kitchen with several glass tumblers and three rose-decorated bowls. Into the glasses he pours vodka, into the bowls, mastova, a rice-based meatball soup laden with freshly foraged oyster mushrooms. A little bowl of live yogurt is also served, as at all meals in Tajikistan, to cut through the oil, cleanse the palate, and aid digestion. As I scrape my bowl clean, Shah is busy with our glasses. "This sprig of ibex grass goes well with this," he says, dropping a few stems into our tumblers of vodka. We clink glasses and cheer "tvoye zdorovye!" in Russian.

He goes on to share a few foraging anecdotes, observing "nature provides, even in this hostile environment." Apricot oil, he tells me, pressed from the fruit's kernel, is mixed by Pamiris with warm milk as a treatment for high blood pressure. Kiboon—an herb with no English name that grows "on the wet side of mountains"—is burned to cleanse houses and is eaten for its vitamin content. Animal fat doubles as sunscreen in hot weather. A single goat skin is sewn up carefully and then inflated and used by children as a raft (locally known as a burdyuk) to cross rivers, which is exactly how Alexander the Great crossed the Oxus (Pamir) River in 329 BC.

Top: Herds of cattle grazing on the Pamir Plateau; Bottom: Mr Parpi Shah, "King of the Mountain Grass"

We slam our glasses down again: First, for the Pamirs, then for Tajikistan, and finally, we toast all mountain travelers.

Standing to leave I give Shah and his son a heartfelt *rakhmat* (thank you). Shah almost blushes and says, "it's nothing, here we help travelers," and he means it too. Life might be tough in the Pamirs, but hospitality is in the blood and religion of Tajiks. The local proverb, *ba labi ob burda tashna overdan* (always bring a thirsty person to the river), says it all.

Right: A lake in the High Pamirs; Below: Curd dried on top of a roof , used in soups during the long winter months in the Pamirs

Apricot and Red Lentil Soup

Serves 4 to 6

3 tablespoons olive oil
1 large onion, finely chopped
1 large carrot, finely chopped
3 garlic cloves, finely chopped
½ cup dried apricots, chopped
1 teaspoon cumin seeds
4 tomatoes, peeled
  and chopped
⅔ cup dried split red lentils
4 cups hot vegetable stock
2 tablespoons thyme leaves
juice of 1 lemon
handful of flat-leaf parsley
  leaves, finely chopped
sea salt and freshly ground
  black pepper

A whole book could be written about apricots in this region. Almost everywhere apricots are dried out across rooftops and are sold fresh at the roadside. In Uzbekistan, the pits are cooked in ash, the shells cracked open, and the kernels sold like nuts. In Tajikistan (which has 300 varieties of apricot), mountain-dwelling folk make noch khurchpa, a simple sunny orange soup comprised of little more than mashed apricots, water, and flour. In Armenia, lentils are added, which gives the soup plenty of body and texture, as here. A meatier version with lamb is sometimes made, too.

Heat the oil in a large pan and cook the onion and carrot until softened and sweet. Add the garlic, apricots, and cumin seeds and cook until fragrant. Stir in the tomatoes and cook for a few minutes more until they start to break down.

Add the red lentils, pour over the stock, and bring to a boil. Reduce the heat and simmer, covered, for 20 minutes until the lentils are tender. Add the thyme leaves and lemon juice and remove from the heat.

Blitz half of the soup in a blender and return to the pan (or use a handheld blender to semi-blend in the pan. Some texture is good here.) Add more liquid if the soup needs thinning, add salt and pepper to taste.

Serve hot with parsley scattered generously into the bowls.

Tajik Green Lentil and Rice Soup

Serves 4

olive oil

1 onion, finely chopped

2 celery stalks, finely chopped

1 carrot, finely chopped

4 tomatoes, chopped

3 garlic cloves, finely chopped

2 teaspoons cumin seeds

½ teaspoon ground allspice

1 cup green or brown lentils, washed

¾ cup brown rice, washed

2 bay leaves

4 cups hot vegetable stock

½ cup crumbly goat cheese

sea salt and freshly ground black pepper

For the herb paste

6 tablespoons olive oil

a good handful of flat-leaf parsley

a good handful of cilantro

a handful of sorrel or mint leaves

a handful of pistachios

squeeze of lemon juice

Fatty meat broths are popular in Tajikistan, so this hearty vegetarian soup is a welcome contrast and a meal in itself. It is thick with rice and lentils, both of which are native to Central Asia. Peppery greens are added at the end, and some form of dairy product will lift the dish. Here, it's finished with a green swirl of herb paste and some crumbled sharp cheese. Alternatively, you could add a dollop of herbed suzma (see page 40) or simply stir in some chopped greens for the final 5 minutes of cooking.

Heat a large saucepan over medium heat and add a good glug of oil. Add in the onion, celery, carrot, and tomato, and cook until softened. Add the garlic, cumin seeds, and allspice. Cook for another minute, then stir in the lentils, rice, and bay leaves.

Pour in the vegetable stock. Bring to a boil, then turn down the heat and cover the pan. Cook for 20 to 30 minutes until the rice and lentils are tender.

Meanwhile, make the herb paste: Put all the ingredients in a small blender with a good pinch of salt and pepper. Blend to a thick purée.

Thin the soup with a little hot water and taste for seasoning. Ladle into serving bowls. Spoon over the herb paste and crumble in the cheese.

Pomegranate Soup

Serves 4

¾ cup yellow split peas
2 tablespoons olive oil
2 onions, finely chopped
4 garlic cloves, finely chopped
1 teaspoon ground turmeric
½ teaspoon chile powder
½ cinnamon stick
4 cups hot vegetable stock
1¾ cups pomegranate juice
2 tablespoons pomegranate
  molasses
sea salt and freshly ground black
  pepper
pinch of sugar (optional)
2 scallions, chopped
3½ ounces spinach leaves,
  coarsely chopped
a handful of flat-leaf parsley,
  coarsely chopped
a handful of cilantro,
  coarsely chopped

To serve
seeds of ½ pomegranate
1 tablespoon mint leaves,
  thinly sliced

This is an Azerbaijani soup with sweet, tart, and complex spice flavors. Substitute the split peas for green or brown lentils if you prefer.

Unless your split peas are very fresh, soak them in cold water overnight.

Heat the oil in a large saucepan over medium heat and soften the onions. Add the garlic and spices, and stir for 1 to 2 minutes until fragrant. Pour in the drained split peas, add the stock and pomegranate juice, and bring to a boil. Cook for 30 to 45 minutes until the split peas are tender. Add more hot water if you want a thinner broth.

Stir in the pomegranate molasses and taste the soup for seasoning. If it is tart, a pinch of sugar will mellow the flavor. Remove the cinnamon stick and add the scallions, spinach, parsley, and cilantro and cook just long enough for them to wilt into the soup. Serve scattered with pomegranate seeds and ribbons of fresh mint.

Winter Kuksu

Serves 4

For the pickled cucumber
2 small Korean cucumbers
  or ½ English cucumber
1 tablespoon sugar
1 teaspoon sea salt

For the beef
10½ ounces beef sirloin or
  tenderloin
2 teaspoons Korean
  chile powder
1 teaspoon sesame oil

For the broth
4 cups hot beef stock
1 tablespoon dark soy sauce
1 tablespoon rice vinegar
2 tablespoons sugar
½ teaspoon sea salt
a small bunch of fresh dill
  fronds, chopped

To serve
4 cups egg noodles, fresh
  or dried
1 tablespoon sesame oil
½ cup kimchi
1 tablespoon sesame seeds,
  toasted

Eaten hot in winter, cold in summer, this noodle soup is one of the most popular Koryo-saram dishes. It is also one where the fusion of East and Central Asian flavors can most clearly be tasted. The sweet, umami-laden beef broth familiar to Korean palates is scented with dill and toasted sesame seeds as a nod to its regional home.

This recipe uses a quick pickled cucumber and kimchi, but you can vary these elements, depending on what you have on hand. Typical additions could include salted radishes, grated beets, stir-fried seasonal vegetables, grilled bell peppers, or hard-boiled eggs. The soup is served with each ingredient arranged separately around the bowl.

For the pickled cucumber, shave the cucumbers into ribbons using a mandolin, or slice into thin discs with a knife. Toss with the sugar and salt, and let pickle for 10 minutes. Rinse off the seasoning and pat dry with paper towels. Taste to check if it needs a little more sweetness or salt.

For the beef, preheat a ridged grill pan. Rub the steak with the chile powder, a little salt, then the sesame oil. When the pan is very hot, sear the steak for 1 to 2 minutes on each side, until done to your liking. Set aside, covered, to rest while you make the broth.

For the broth, heat the stock in a large pan and add all its aromatics. Taste to check the balance of flavors and adjust accordingly for sweetness, saltiness, or tang.

Cook the noodles according to the package instructions. Drain and toss with the sesame oil. Mound a nest of noodles into the middle of four serving bowls and ladle over the hot broth. Slice the beef and pile onto one side of each bowl, drizzling with any meaty juices. Fill the remaining two-thirds of each bowl with a tangle of pickled cucumber and another of kimchi. Finally, sprinkle with the sesame seeds before serving.

To Kashgar for far-flung noodles

"Travels, like a wise man, help you appreciate both the big and the little."
Local saying, Xinjiang, China

It is market day, shortly after daybreak, and there are boys selling cherry-red pomegranates, and old ladies with baked discs of non bread artfully wrapped in blankets to keep them warm and fresh. Tables buckle under the weight of enormous fuzzy-skinned peaches, while bubbling cauldrons of plov cast long shadows over skewered shashlik on hot charcoal that crackle deliciously in the air.

This could be at any market in Central Asia, but in fact it's the Sunday bazaar in Kashgar, in the far west of China, possibly the most fascinating city in all Asia to watch locals shop and eat. Traders have been eating at this dusty oasis for hundreds of years. Caravans would stop off here as they traveled west to Europe via Samarkand. It was a welcome stop on a section of the Silk Road ringed by some of the highest mountains on earth, which also shoulders the forbidding Taklamakan Desert (known to the Chinese as the "desert of death").

Geographically, this ancient crossroads lies in China, but its heart and soul are Central Asian. Kashgar's native inhabitants may be citizens of the People's Republic of China, but they are Uighurs. Their language is Turkic, their ancestors are Turkic, and they hold deep Islamic beliefs. Facially, they look more like their Kazakh and Mongol neighbors, not the Han Chinese.

As the market scene unfolds, subtle cultural differences between the Uighur and Han Chinese start to emerge. Uighurs stoop to hoover up noodles from their bowls, unlike the Han who raise noodle bowls to their lips. Uighur dumplings, like the non bread, are baked; Chinese dumplings are more often steamed. Butchers hawk halal mutton and lamb, rather than pork, catering to their Muslim Uighur customers. Noodles are always made fresh by the Uighur, whereas the Han tend to buy them.

Traders, sporting black, square Uzbek-style skullcaps, sell silky ikat cloth by the foot. The fiercest bartering takes place over horses and Karakul lambskins. The heartfelt Muslim greeting of *"es salaam aleikum"* (peace be upon you) is the common greeting here rather than the cheery Mandarin *"ni hao"* (hello). Between sales, the traders sip rough black chai and smoke coarse tobacco rolled in the pages of old books.

Age-old techniques persist here. Corn grinding is done on a spinning millstone driven by a water-powered wheel—a method that has not changed in centuries. Bakers crouch over a huge round-mouthed tandoor oven, pressing balls of dough to bake on its piping-hot stone walls.

Acrobats and magicians jostle for the crowd's attention, but the noodle stalls are the best spectacle of all. Over a flour-dusted table, Uighur cooks take a pillow of kneaded dough to craft a long rope. Then, holding one end in each hand, they swing it like a jump rope until it is stretched ever longer. Once the rope is about 5 feet in length, the cook doubles the dough back on itself and the flinging action is repeated, cat's-cradle-like, until there are many thin strands. Finally, the noodles are mixed with a meat broth, peppers, onions, and tomatoes, creating a dish known as laghman (see page 58 for our version of lamb and noodle laghman).

Second in the photogenic stakes is *apke*, or goat's head soup. A quick peek inside the cauldron will reveal a goat's head atop a mound of cleaned intestines that have been stuffed with eggs and meat—a nutritious lunch for the culinary adventurer.

For visitors, there's one must-know tip, and that is what *"posh, posh!"* means. Ignore the command to "move out of the way!" and you risk being mowed down by an angry speeding horseman and his cart of wobbling cabbages.

Top: Noodle maker at the Sunday market, Kashgar, Xinjiang, China: Bottom: Carts along the road

Lamb and Noodle Laghman

Serves 4

3 tablespoons sunflower oil

1¼ pounds boneless leg of lamb, cut into strips

1 onion, sliced

1 red bell pepper, seeded and cut into strips

2 tomatoes, seeded and chopped

1 turnip, peeled and cut into strips

1 red chile, seeded and sliced

2 garlic cloves, sliced

2 tablespoons tomato paste

sea salt

4 cups hot lamb or beef stock

2 star anise

1 cinnamon stick

2 tablespoons rice vinegar or cider vinegar

14 ounces fresh or dried wheat noodles

2 scallions, finely sliced

a small handful of cilantro, finely chopped

a small handful of basil leaves, cut into ribbons

To serve

1 tablespoon dried chile flakes

2 teaspoons ground sumac

Laghman, one of the most ubiquitous dishes in Central Asia, actually originates from far west China, home to the Muslim Uighur people. It has roots as the Chinese dish Lo Mein, in which noodles are usually tossed with umami-sauced meat.

Laghman has two parts. The first is a fragrant lamb stew, or *vadzha*, which can be made in advance, and indeed improves by doing do. Second—and key—are the noodles, ideally fresh, hand-flung noodles that require a simple pasta dough but a highly skilled technique. (Take a look at a video online if you want to attempt making them at home, or seek out home-style Chinese noodles or udon noodles as a substitute.) A final flourish of cilantro and basil, and a heady mixture of chile flakes and sumac added at the table, make laghman addictively good.

Heat a wok over high heat and add the oil. Add the lamb and stir-fry quickly to brown the meat. Add the onion, bell pepper, tomatoes, turnip, chile, and garlic and stir-fry for a few minutes until softened.

Stir in the tomato paste and season with salt. Add the lamb stock, star anise, and cinnamon stick. Bring to a simmer and cook for 45 minutes. Add the vinegar and taste for seasoning. If making in advance, chill now and gently reheat before serving.

Cook the noodles in salted boiling water. Drain and add a tangle to each bowl. Ladle over the meat, vegetables, and broth. Scatter the scallions, cilantro, and basil over the top.

Serve with a little bowl of chile flakes mixed with ground sumac for diners to add at the table according to taste.

Kazan Kebab

Serves 4

14 ounces stew beef, cut
   into cubes
1 tablespoon all-purpose flour
sea salt and freshly ground
   black pepper
2 tablespoon clarified butter
   or sunflower oil
3 garlic cloves, crushed
2 cups tomato sauce
1 bay leaf
1 (14-ounce) can chickpeas,
   drained and rinsed
a small bunch of cilantro,
   leaves torn
1 tablespoon torn basil leaves
1 tablespoon fresh oregano
   leaves
1 tablespoon chopped dill
   fronds
juice of ½ lemon

To serve
lemon wedges
sliced fresh chile

In most of Uzbekistan, the name of this dish refers
to lamb cooked with potatoes in a *kazan* (a large
wok-like pan). However, in the Fergana Valley (a
fertile region that straddles Uzbekistan, Tajikistan,
and Kyrgyzstan) a kazan kebab is the name of a
delicious hearty meat and chickpea soup. This
is home cooking, not something you'll find in
restaurants.

Toss the beef in the flour and season with salt and pepper. Heat
the clarified butter in a large casserole pan or Dutch oven and
brown the beef, in batches if necessary. Add the garlic and cook,
stirring, for a couple of minutes, then add the tomato sauce, bay
leaf, and 2 cups of cold water. Bring to a boil, then turn down the
heat and cover the pan. Simmer for 1 hour, stirring occasionally,
or until the meat is tender.

Stir in the chickpeas, herbs, and lemon juice, and taste for
seasoning. Simmer for another 10 minutes before serving with
wedges of lemon and sliced chile to add at the table.

Roast Meats
& Kebabs

Sun, sand, and sour cherries on Central Asia's beach

The smell of smoky spiced mutton and vinegary onions drifts out of makeshift yurt cafes, suggesting a brisk trade in shashlik. By the shoreline of this vast, mountain-fringed stretch of saline water, pedalos bob gently on pale blue waves and paragliders take off into a cloudless sky. After too long spent trundling through Central Asia's mountains aboard dusty buses, life looks sweet on the beach. It matters not at all that I'm in landlocked Kyrgyzstan, because this "beach" lies on the shore of Lake Issyk-Kul, one of the world's largest alpine lakes.

I breathe in a lungful of clean air and stretch out my towel along with hundreds of Kazakh, Russian, and Kyrgyz tourists. Collectively, our faces soften in the sun as we suck sour cherries and surrender ourselves to the cooling effects of Baltika beer. Only the backdrop of chocolate-brown mountains hint at our altitude—almost 5,300 feet—as they tremble, mirage-like, under a fiery sun.

Issyk-Kul sits squarely in remotest Central Asia and after a long, hard winter people flock to its shoreline, crying out for a healthy dose of sun and sand.

Since the end of the Soviet era (1922–91), Cholpon Ata, the resort on Issyk-Kul's northern shore, has been known as the ultimate summer destination for thousands of holidaymakers from Russia and Kazakhstan. It remains a place of simple pleasures, one of buckets and shovels, sandcastles, and blow-up beach balls.

Enjoying life on the beach here is nothing new. As long ago as the fourteenth century, the ruthless Asian conqueror, Tamerlane—who now rests in Samarkand's Gur-e-Amir—had a castle overlooking the relaxing scene at Issyk-Kul. During the Soviet era, Communist Party cadres would arrive to exchange their putyovka (vouchers) for a restorative break at a sanatorium. Russian cosmonauts also convalesced here: locals proudly inform visitors that the first man in space, Yuri Gagarin, holidayed here after his historic flight. And who could blame him? Issyk-Kul's lapping waves and craggy mountain views make for a fine place to come down to earth.

On the main street, a 10-minute walk from the beach, a string of restaurants and stolovaya (basic cafes) cater to hordes of hungry vacationers eager for plates of fatty shashlik, fluffy piles of mutton plov, and bowls of magenta-colored borscht. Fueled by the somewhat hedonistic atmosphere—not common in Kyrgyzstan—men chase their kazy (horsemeat sausages) with half-tumblers of samogon, homemade vodka, or moonshine, which is lethally strong. One of my fellow diners tells me that she and her family had never tasted fresh peaches until yesterday, "in Siberia we only have cans, they are nothing like the fresh ones here," she said.

Every year, during the short summer (mid-July to mid-August), dozens of guesthouses open their doors to these tourists. The owners, who live off their summer earnings, know exactly what the vacationers desire. They come for lace tablecloths, rustic bungalows, and backyard orchards. And meal times with home-cooked laghman (mutton stew with noodles, shredded cabbage, and onion) and syrniki (pancakes) slathered with sour cream and fresh blackcurrant jam. Come the summer, it is virtually impossible to bag a decent komnat (spare room) close to the lake.

Top: Girl selling kumis—fermented mare's milk and other drinks;
Bottom: Beach on Lake Issyk-Kul, Kyrgystan

Chicken Shashlik with Pink Onions and Pomegranate

Serves 4

For the chicken shashlik
8 to 12 chicken thighs, skinless
  and boneless
2 tablespoons mayonnaise
5 garlic cloves, crushed
zest and juice of 1 lemon
1 teaspoon paprika
½ teaspoon ground cumin
½ teaspoon sea salt
½ teaspoon black pepper

sunflower oil, for grilling

**For the pink onions and
pomegranate**
2 white onions
½ cup red wine vinegar
2 tablespoons sugar
½ tablespoon sea salt
1 pomegranate

non bread, to serve
  (see page 152)

Tangles of paper-thin raw onion accompany kebabs of all forms in Uzbekistan. Here a quick pickling takes away the raw astringency, leaving the onion sweet and tangy with bursts of tart pomegranate. A perfect match for charred, garlicky morsels of chicken.

Cut the chicken thighs into chunks, removing any fat or sinew as you go. Mix the remaining ingredients together to make a marinade and toss with the chicken. Cover and leave in the fridge for a few hours or overnight. If you are using wooden rather than metal skewers, put them in water to soak at this stage, which will keep them from burning when you cook.

To prepare the onions, slice into very thin half-moons with a sharp knife. Shake together the vinegar, sugar, and salt in a screw-top jar until dissolved. Add the onion and let steep at room temperature for 10 minutes.

Drain off the vinegar, squeezing out as much liquid as you can, then transfer the pink-tinged onions to a bowl. Scatter with the seeds and juice of the pomegranate.

When you are ready to start cooking, thread the chicken pieces onto the skewers. Preheat a grill pan over high heat and brush with oil. Grill the kebabs for 10 to 15 minutes, turning occasionally, until cooked through and charred. Serve with the onions and non bread.

Roast Lamb with a Sticky Pomegranate Glaze

Serves 6

3¼ pounds lamb shoulder,
  on the bone
3 garlic cloves
2 red onions, thickly sliced
seeds of 2 pomegranates

For the glaze

¼ cup pomegranate molasses
¼ cup honey
1 tablespoon sunflower oil
1 green chile, sliced
1½ teaspoons ground
  coriander
1½ teaspoons ground cinnamon
1½ teaspoons ground
  cardamom
1 teaspoon sea salt
½ teaspoon ground black
  pepper

The influence of Persian flavors is evident in Tajik food—demonstrated in this recipe with the pomegranate, honey, and spices. In Tajikistan, following a feast like this, the diners' preferred expression of merriment is to dance, not drink, the night away.

Remove the lamb from the fridge 1 to 2 hours before you start cooking to bring it to room temperature. Preheat the oven to 325°F.

Use the tip of a sharp knife to make deep slits into the lamb. Cut the garlic lengthwise into fat matchsticks and poke them into the slits. Put the onions in the bottom of a roasting pan and sit the shoulder on top.

Mix all the ingredients for the glaze together and pour over the lamb. Pour a small cupful of cold water into the bottom of the roasting pan and cover the whole thing with a tent of aluminum foil, making sure it is well sealed. Roast for 4 hours, then remove the foil—the meat should be almost falling off the bone. Baste the lamb with the juices.

Turn the oven up to 400°F and continue to cook, uncovered, for another 30 minutes, basting again halfway through, to brown and glaze the meat.

Skim off as much fat as possible from the pan. Pour any remaining juices over the lamb along with the sticky onions—you might need to add a splash of hot water to loosen the precious sticky bits from the pan. Sprinkle with the ruby-red pomegranate seeds before serving. A mound of buttered rice or spiced roast potatoes makes a good accompaniment.

Slow-roast Mutton with Sultan's Delight

Serves 4 to 6

For the mutton

17 tablespoons (2 sticks + 1 tablespoon) unsalted butter, softened

1 teaspoon sea salt

1 teaspoon ground cumin

1 teaspoon ground cinnamon

½ teaspoon cayenne pepper

½ teaspoon caraway seeds

4 garlic cloves, crushed

1 shoulder of mutton on the bone (about 5½ pounds)

12 shallots, peeled and halved

2 heads of garlic, unpeeled and halved across the center

For the sultan's delight

2 eggplants

olive oil, for rubbing

2 tablespoons butter

3 tablespoons all-purpose flour

1 cup milk

¾ cup hard cheese (such as Cheddar), grated

pinch of grated nutmeg

The dish that so delighted the Ottoman Sultan Murad IV back in the seventeenth century was a silky mound of cheesy eggplant purée—hunkar begendi. If you don't incline toward roast mutton, it is equally enchanting served with lamb chops.

Preheat to oven to 275°F.

Make a spice paste for the mutton by blending together the butter, salt, spices, and crushed garlic. Slather this all over the meat. Put the shallots and garlic halves in a deep roasting pan and sit the mutton on top. Pour in 3 cups of cold water, or enough to come up to the bottom of the meat. Cover the top with aluminum foil and cook in the oven for 6 hours, or until the meat is completely tender.

While the mutton is cooking, prepare the sultan's delight. Put the whole eggplants in a separate roasting pan, drizzle with a little olive oil, and transfer to the oven with the lamb. Cook for 1 hour, or until softened. Let cool.

Melt the butter in a pan over low heat. Add the flour and stir continuously until the mixture turns pale golden. Take the pan off the heat and add the milk, slowly at first, making sure the liquid is well mixed in before you add more. Return to the heat and bring to a boil, stirring continuously until the sauce has thickened. Turn the heat down and let simmer for 5 minutes. Stir in the cheese and nutmeg.

Peel the eggplant and put the pulp in a strainer. Gently squeeze out any liquid. Add the eggplant to the cheese sauce and taste for seasoning.

When the meat is tender, remove the foil, turn the oven up to 400°F, and brown the meat for 20 minutes. Rest the meat and strain the juices into a saucepan and reduce a little. Serve the mutton with the sultan's delight and the pan juices.

An obsession with eggplants

As the early evening sun balances on the Bosphorus, the aroma of patlican biber drifts lazily from kitchen windows. This is the ubiquitous dish of eggplants and green bell peppers fried in olive oil, and to me this alluring smell *is* Istanbul.

In Turkey, the eggplant is known as the sultan of vegetables and it is brilliantly versatile. When cooked, the tight, shiny, purple-black skins open to reveal a subtle, savory, and silky flesh that is made for soaking up salt, sauce, and olive oil. Throughout the country, eggplants are grilled, speared onto kebabs, pulped into soups and dips, whipped into sauces, and stuffed with rice, bulgur wheat, ground meat, and spices. Step into any market—and this is true throughout most of Central Asia and the Caucasus too—and you'll never be far from an eggplant. The biggest eggplants I ever saw were in Baku in Azerbaijan, where they were the size of rugby balls, but to my mind the smaller ones tend to have the best flavor.

Restaurants all over Turkey serve a plethora of eggplant-based dishes. Some of the tastiest to look out for are kopoglu (fried eggplant with yogurt and tomato sauce) and the decadently smooth purée, hunkar begendi, which translates as sultan's delight. All of these benefit from the company of the red wine from Cappadocia, an ice-cold Efes beer or anise-flavored raki, the local brandy, which is often served with a meze. Come to think of it, you could enjoy a Turkish gastronomic journey pegged entirely around the eggplant—seeking out kizartma, a fried eggplant, pepper, and potato dish topped with a rich thick tomato sauce, in Bodrum or sourcing watermelon and eggplant jam (yes, really!) in Antalya.

Grilled Lamb Kebabs with Cinnamon, Cloves, and Hot Hummus

Serves 4

For the kebabs

1¼ pounds boneless leg of lamb
⅓ cup olive oil
3 tablespoons lemon juice
1 onion, grated
1 garlic clove, crushed
1 bay leaf
1 teaspoon ground cinnamon
½ teaspoon ground clove
½ teaspoon ground black
  pepper
½ teaspoon sea salt

For the hot hummus

1 (14-ounce) can chickpeas,
  drained and rinsed
2 teaspoons tahini
1 garlic clove, crushed
2 tablespoons lemon juice
1 teaspoon Turkish red pepper
  or Aleppo pepper
½ teaspoon ground cinnamon
½ teaspoon sea salt
3 tablespoons extra virgin olive
  oil, plus extra to drizzle
1 tablespoon pine nuts

To serve

lemon wedges
pita bread

Hummus is often served hot in Turkey; heating it in the oven slightly soufflés it. I recommend scooping up the charred morsels of meat and hot hummus with pita bread.

Cut the lamb into generous cubes, removing any fat or sinew.

Make a marinade for the lamb by combining all the remaining ingredients in a large freezer bag. Add the meat, seal the bag, and massage the cubes through the bag to thoroughly coat them in the marinade. Leave in the fridge overnight, or up to 24 hours.

To prepare the hummus, put the chickpeas, tahini, garlic, lemon juice, spices, and salt in a food processor. Add a couple of tablespoons of cold water and turn on the food processor. Slowly trickle in the olive oil with the motor running. Blend for a few minutes until smooth. Spoon the hummus into a small ovenproof dish. Scatter with the pine nuts and drizzle with olive oil. It will keep in the fridge for a few days, until you are ready to serve.

Preheat the oven to 400°F.

Heat the hummus in the oven for 10 minutes while you cook the lamb.

Thread the lamb onto metal skewers. Preheat a grill pan over high heat, or use a barbecue. Grill the lamb for 3 to 5 minutes on each side, or until cooked to your liking. Serve with the hot hummus, wedges of lemon, and perhaps some toasted pita bread.

Thunderstone Lamb Chops with Sour Cherry Sauce

Serves 4

For the sour cherry sauce
1 cup sour cherries, pitted
  and chopped
juice of ½ lemon
1 tablespoon sugar
½ teaspoon ground cinnamon
½ teaspoon ground black
  pepper
pinch of ground clove

For the lamb
8 trimmed lamb chops
sunflower oil, for cooking
sea salt and freshly ground
  black pepper

shots of cherry vodka,
  to serve

In the remote mountains of Azerbaijan, resourceful people, lacking cooking utensils, once cooked their meat between hot stones. Not just any stone: apparently they would select stones weathered by thunderstorms, which somehow made them stronger. First heated then rubbed with animal fat, the stones sandwiched the meat to cook it quickly on both sides. A similar effect can be achieved at home using two hot pans, one that fits inside the other.

If you can't find sour cherries, use sweet cherries, omit the sugar, and add a little more lemon juice. A shot of cherry vodka alongside makes the perfect pairing.

First make the sauce: Put all the ingredients in a pan and cook gently for 10 minutes until the cherries have broken down. Set aside to cool to room temperature.

Remove the thick layer of fat from around the lamb chops, then lay them between two sheets of plastic wrap. Use a rolling pin to beat out and flatten the meat a little. Rub the chops with a little oil on both sides, then season with salt and lots of black pepper.

You'll need two pans, one a large frying pan and the other a heavy, flat-based pan that will fit into the frying pan, ideally cast iron. Preheat both pans until very hot. Put the chops into the frying pan and put the hot base of the second pan on top. Weigh down the pan with a couple of unopened cans and leave the chops to cook through to your liking, about 4 minutes for medium-rare.

Let rest for 5 minutes before serving with the cherry sauce and shots of clear cherry vodka.

Chapli Kebabs

Serves 6

**For the tomato and
pomegranate relish**
6 very ripe plum tomatoes
seeds of 1 pomegranate
1 green chile, seeded and
  finely chopped
a handful of cilantro,
  finely chopped
a few mint leaves, finely sliced
1 garlic clove, crushed
1 teaspoon sugar
1 teaspoon sea salt
juice of ½ lemon

For the kebabs
2 onions, coarsely chopped
2 cloves garlic, crushed
1 knob of ginger (about the size
  of your thumb), peeled and
  grated
2 green chiles, seeded
a small bunch of cilantro
1¾ pounds ground beef
2 tablespoons ground coriander
2 teaspoons ground cumin
2 teaspoons garam masala
1 teaspoon sea salt
seeds of 1 pomegranate
sunflower oil, for cooking

To serve
lime wedges
non bread (see page 152)

**These Afghan spiced beef patties are so named
from their flat shape, resembling a sandal, or *chapli*.
The meat is charred on the outside, juicy within,
and jeweled with pomegranate seeds.**

First make the relish: Cut the tomatoes into quarters and remove
the watery seeds. Dice the flesh as finely as you can. Stir in the
remaining ingredients and let marinate until you are ready to eat.

To make the kebabs, put the onions, garlic, ginger, chiles, and
cilantro in a food processor. Pulse until finely chopped, but not
to a paste. Add the beef, spices, and salt, and pulse just to bring
everything together.

Transfer the meat to a clean surface and use your hands to mix
in the pomegranate seeds. Form the meat into six large patties,
about ¾-inch thick and, for authenticity, the shape of a sandal.

Heat a little oil in a large frying pan. Cook the patties, in batches,
for 2 minutes, or until browned on the bottom. Flip and cook for
1 to 2 minutes longer, or until cooked through to your liking.
Serve with wedges of lime, non bread, and the tomato and
pomegranate relish.

Beef Shashlik with Tahini and Pistachio Sauce

Serves 4

For the sauce

1 ounce country bread (about
   1 slice), crust removed
¾ cup shelled pistachios
1 small garlic clove, crushed
1 tablespoons tahini
juice of 1 lemon
1 tablespoon olive oil
sea salt and freshly ground
   black pepper

For the kebabs

1¼ pounds ground beef
1 red onion, grated
1 garlic clove, crushed
¾ cup shelled pistachios,
   coarsely chopped
2 teaspoons fresh thyme
   leaves
2 teaspoons ground cumin
½ teaspoon cayenne pepper
½ teaspoon ground allspice
1 teaspoon sea salt
1 tablespoon olive oil

flatbread, to serve

In the province of Gazientep, in Turkey's southeastern Anatolia region, pistachios (*sam fıstığı*) are so celebrated that an arts festival is held in their name. The nuts define the region's food, from the glorious green baklava to these shashlik, meat kebabs studded with pistachios. They can be made with beef or lamb.

For the sauce, soak the bread in a bowl of cold water for a few minutes, then squeeze out as much of the water as possible. Put into a food processor with the pistachios and process to a paste. Add the remaining ingredients and blend again. Add enough cold water to thin the sauce to a smooth, dropping consistency. Season with salt and pepper and refrigerate until needed, but bring to room temperature before serving.

For the kebabs, put all the ingredients, except the olive oil, into a large bowl. Use your hands to mix everything until smooth. Divide the mixture into eight pieces and shape each into a long, thin sausage around a metal skewer.

Preheat a grill pan over high heat. Brush the shashlik with olive oil and cook for 5 to 10 minutes, turning occasionally, until well-browned and cooked through to your liking. Serve with the pistachio sauce and some warm flatbread.

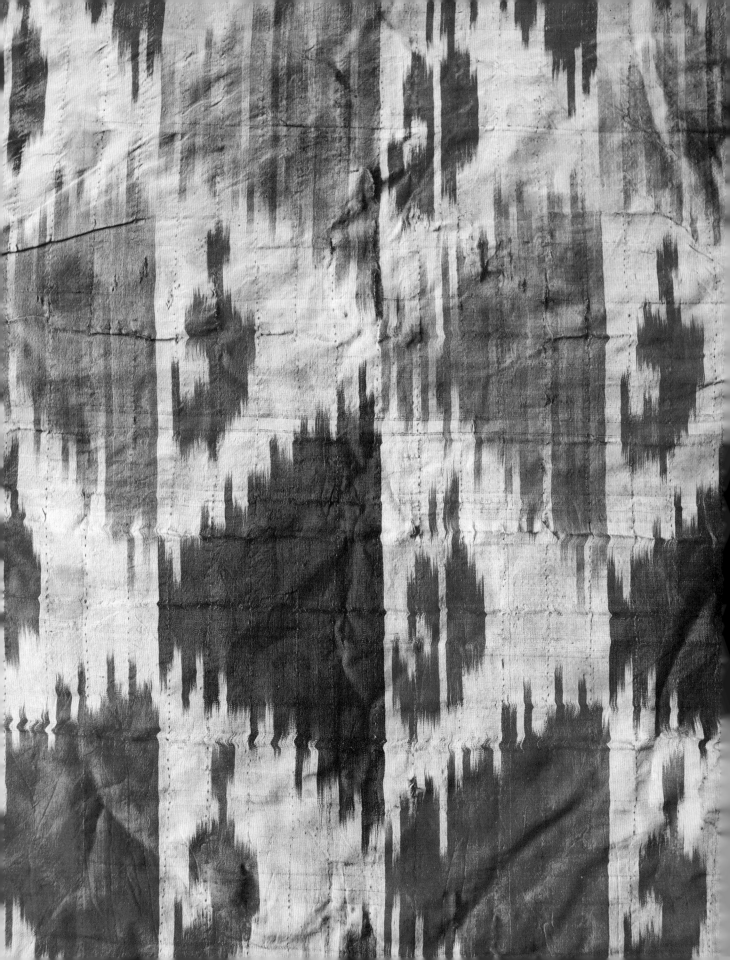

Warming Food
for Long Winters

Salmon Kulebyaka

Serves 6

3 tablespoons butter

10½ ounces boneless, skinless salmon fillets

1 onion, finely chopped

1 teaspoon coriander seeds

1 teaspoon cumin seeds

½ teaspoon ground turmeric

seeds of 2 green cardamom pods

2 cups mushrooms, sliced

zest of 1 lemon

3 tablespoons chopped fresh flat-leaf parsley leaves

3 tablespoons chopped dill fronds

sea salt and freshly ground black pepper

½ cup cooked basmati rice

18 ounces puff pastry

3 hard-boiled eggs, peeled and sliced

1 egg, beaten

For the sauce

5 tablespoons butter

juice of 1 lemon

2 teaspoons chopped dill fronds

In Russia, pies (pirogi) come in many shapes and sizes. Sometimes the dough is leavened, other times not, while the pie may be open or closed. Inside the pie—which could be triangular, round, or square—you'll find fillings ranging from meat and mushrooms to cabbage and cheese. One of the very finest is the kulebyaka (or *coulibiac* in French), a fully enclosed salmon and rice pie—robust, golden-brown, and crusty. It can be made well in advance.

Melt half the butter in a frying pan over medium heat and cook the salmon fillets for 2 to 3 minutes on each side. Lift out the fillets and set aside to cool. Add the remaining butter to the pan and cook the onion for 10 minutes until soft and turning golden. Stir in the spices and mushrooms, and cook for 5 minutes. Remove from the heat and let cool before stirring in the lemon zest, herbs, salt, and pepper. Finally add the cooked rice and mix through gently.

To make the pie, roll out the puff pastry to a 16-inch square. Cut it into two pieces, one slightly wider than the other. Line a baking sheet with parchment and lay the narrower strip of pastry on it. Spoon over two-thirds of the rice mixture, leaving a border. Flake over the salmon, top with the egg slices, and then the remaining rice.

Brush a little beaten egg over the pastry border. Drape the larger piece of pastry over the top and press the edges to seal the two sheets together, crimping with your fingers or pressing down with the tines of a fork. Score the top with the back of a knife or prick with a non bread stamp, then glaze with beaten egg. This can now be chilled until you are ready to cook.

Preheat the oven to 425°F. Bake for 25 to 30 minutes until golden brown. Let rest for 10 minutes before slicing thickly to serve.

To make the sauce, melt the butter and add the lemon juice and dill. Bring a bowl of the buttery sauce to the table to drizzle over the kulebyaka.

Pan-fried Trout with Green Garlic Sauce

Serves 4

For the green garlic sauce
1 fat garlic clove
½ teaspoon sea salt
1¾ cups cilantro leaves, finely chopped

For the fish
4 fillets of rainbow trout or other freshwater fish (about 3½ ounces each)
olive oil, for frying
sea salt and freshly ground black pepper

Even though meat rules the Central Asian table, the lakes and rivers that crisscross the region yield an abundance of freshwater fish, eaten mainly in the cold winter months. In this recipe, the trout is cooked first then doused in its grassy green marinade. This reversal of the typical order allows the raw garlic to keep its pungency.

Start by making the sauce: Using a mortar and pestle, pound the garlic with the salt to a smooth paste. Add the cilantro and continue pounding to produce a vivid green paste. Thin with ½ cup of cold water.

Season the trout fillets with salt and pepper. Heat ½-inch of oil in a frying pan over medium–high heat. When the oil starts to shimmer, add the fillets, skin-side down, and cook for 4 minutes, or until the skin is crisp and golden and the flesh almost cooked through. Turn and cook for another minute before removing the pan from the heat and setting aside to rest; the residual heat of the pan will cook the fillets through. Drizzle with the green garlic sauce while the trout is still warm, which will help it soak up the flavors. Cool to room temperature before serving.

Lazy Cabbage Rolls

Serves 4

olive oil, for frying

1 onion, finely chopped

1 large carrot, grated

⅓ head white of cabbage, finely shredded

1 tablespoon paprika

½ teaspoon caraway seeds

1¼ pounds ground pork

½ cup long-grain rice

1 egg

2 cups tomato sauce

juice of 1 lemon

2 garlic cloves, crushed

½ teaspoon ground allspice

sea salt

pinch of sugar

sour cream, to serve

Cabbage rolls, or golubtsy, are the dish that most Russians associate with childhood dinners with Grandma. Widely made across Central Asia, they are similar to dolmas, except cabbage leaves are used instead of vine leaves.

Beef, lamb, or pork can be used, and the flavors vary from region to region, family to family. The Mountain Jews of Azerbaijan, for example, add cilantro and sour green plums. In Uzbekistan, it is common to have different baked vegetables all stuffed with the same filling. I favor this lazy version where the cabbage leaves are mixed into spiced pork meatballs instead of carefully wrapped around them—hence their affectionate nickname—without compromising on flavor.

Heat a splash of oil in a large lidded frying pan, add the onion and carrot, and cook over medium heat to soften. Throw in the cabbage, cover, and cook until collapsed and tender. Remove the lid, stir in the paprika and caraway seeds, and continue to cook until any liquid has steamed away.

Put the cooked vegetables in a large bowl with the ground pork, rice, and egg. Season generously. Using your hands, mix everything together and form into flattened meatballs. You should get about 16. Put in the fridge for 30 minutes to firm up.

Mix together the tomato sauce, lemon juice, garlic, and allspice. Season with salt and a pinch of sugar.

Wipe out the frying pan and heat a little more oil. In two batches, cook the meatballs for 3 minutes on each side, until golden. Return all the meatballs in one crowded layer and pour over the tomato sauce. Bring to a gentle bubble, then cover, lower the heat, and simmer for 30 minutes, or until the meat is cooked through, the rice is tender, and the tomato sauce is slightly reduced. Serve with a cooling dollop of smetana (sour cream).

Buckwheat Kasha with Caramelized Mushrooms

Serves 4 to 6

1 cup buckwheat groats

3 pats of butter

sunflower oil

2 cups chicken or vegetable
  stock

sea salt and freshly ground
  black pepper

2 onions, chopped

9 ounces chestnut mushrooms,
  sliced

a handful of dill fronds, chopped

a handful of flat-leaf parsley
  leaves, finely chopped

sour cream, to serve

Healthy kasha is the foundation of Russian cuisine. It is best described as a porridge, usually made from toasted buckwheat. It can be sweet or savory and used to be made in huge clay pots all over the Russian countryside. Gluten-free and insanely good for you, children are told "eat your kasha and you will grow up to be as strong as Bogatyr" (Bogatyr being a folk hero similar to a knight).

Kasha has a strong, nutty, almost bitter taste, so it stands up well to other robust flavors. Here, the meaty mushrooms and sweetness from the onion make it ideal for a healthy lunch or side dish. Make more than you need as it keeps well in the fridge for a few days and is just as good cold.

Unless you have bought toasted buckwheat, toast it first: Heat a small pat of the butter and a slick of oil in a saucepan and toast the buckwheat until golden and fragrant.

Meanwhile, bring the stock to a boil. Pour the hot stock over the buckwheat—carefully as it will splatter. Season, turn the heat to low, and cover the pan. Cook for 15 minutes, then remove from the heat. Lightly fluff the grains with a fork, then replace the lid and let steam, off the heat, for another 5 minutes.

While the buckwheat is cooking, heat a large pat of butter and another slick of oil in a large frying pan over medium heat. Add the onions and cook for about 15 minutes, stirring often, until very well softened and starting to turn golden. Add the mushrooms and stir often. At first they will give out water, but keep cooking until this has evaporated and the mushrooms and onions are well caramelized. Season with salt, pepper, and stir in the fresh herbs.

Finally, toss in the buckwheat and allow to warm through with another pat of butter. Serve with sour cream.

Eating with the Mountain Jews of Azerbaijan

At first glance, Gyrmyzy Gasaba is just another small wind-blown town in northern Azerbaijan. Hidden in the shadows of the Caucasus Mountains that separate it from the Russian republic of Dagestan, the town sits high above the rock-strewn banks of the Qudiyalcay River. Beaten-up Ladas line the streets nose to tail, shops display trays of sticky diamond-shaped baklava in their windows, and watermelons are piled up at the roadside. Men play nard, Persian backgammon, under shady trees and in the main park, a statue of former President Heydar Aliyev stands next to a blue, red, and green Azeri flag.

Then, clues to the town's true identity start to appear: a silver menorah here, a Star of David there. Azerbaijan might be a Shia Muslim country, but Gyrmyzy Gasaba is considered to be the world's last surviving shtetl (pre-Holocaust Jewish village). Its sheer isolation has perfectly preserved its traditions, making it a truly unusual destination to visit.

In Yiddish "shtetl" simply means "town," but in the collective Jewish imagination the word is laced with nostalgia. For many Jews, the word recalls traditional but hardscrabble Russian or eastern European villages, like the one depicted in the hit musical *Fiddler on the Roof*.

Walking the Sunday-quiet streets in the center of town I am first struck by its sleepiness. Men shuffle past me, shaking hands with one another and offering each other a "shalom" or "salaam" to Muslims from neighboring towns—religious harmony in action. Locals here take great pride in being the descendants of the first Jews who traveled to Dagestan, Chechnya, and Azerbaijan via Persia (Iran), where they had lived as Jewry following their exile from Israel. Fleeing from forcible conversion by warring Arabs in the eighth century, they left Persia and sought shelter in the remote Caucasus Mountains. They have remained here ever since. The community has long been known as "Mountain Jews," who consider themselves quite separate from the world's two major ethnic Jewish groups—Ashkenazi and Sephardi. For some, Gyrmyzy Gasaba is "Little Jerusalem," possibly the only all-Jewish town outside Israel.

Turning on to Isaak Xanukov Street, I follow my nose, picking up some alluring smells—turmeric, eggs, roast chicken, and chestnuts—to the Bet Knesset synagogue. Once inside the synagogue, the soft aroma of warm fadi (a sweet round bread usually served with black tea) spills into the rug-lined corridor from a little kitchen at the back.

This kitchen is where Naomi Ruvinova cooks for the Sabbath and special occasions. She tells me she's been expecting me and has been cooking all morning to give me a taste of what the Mountain Jews of Azerbaijan like to eat. Her tiny feet, clad in glittery shoes, move fast while my brain tries to compute the complexities of her kitchen alchemy. Agreeing to my offer of help, she hands me a spoon and a handful of raisins to stir into a cauldron of plov. Azerbaijan is home to dozens of different plov recipes. Typically, plov is made with lamb in Azerbaijan, but Ruvinova's is lighter and vegetarian. A small slick of corn oil has colored the rice a sunshine yellow, while a sprinkling of juicy apricots and sweet chestnuts lifts it from the doldrums, turning it into a dish for all the senses. While the plov takes on the flavor of the raisins, she presents a plate of steaming yakhny—a soul-food soup of onions, eggs, veal, and tomatoes—and places it on the table. It is filling mountain food, prepared from simple ingredients, designed to keep the cold at bay.

While I enjoy the warming yakhny, my eyes are drawn toward a plate of hasavyurt on the counter. Ruvinova tells me that this paste-like dip, usually served as a side dish, is made with ground walnuts, red apples, and grape juice, nothing else. I scoop a little onto a Matza

Naomi Ruvinova and the synagogue at Gyrmyzy Gasaba, Azerbaijan

cracker and when I bite into it I find its taste seductive, not-too-sweet, and bright as a summer's day. Plump from sunshine, the cooked apples are so intense in flavor their Western equivalents seem tasteless in comparison.

Then, a little plate of glistening Russian-style golubtsy—cabbage rolls—beckons. Popular here since the Soviet era, Mountain Jews follow the standard recipe, using cabbage leaves to wrap the ingredients, but add an unorthodox sprinkling of cilantro, some acidic green plums, and tomato paste. Sour plums are popular with Jews across the border in Georgia too, where they are added to chakapuli, a lamb and tarragon stew.

Next, Ruvinova lifts her khoyagusht from the oven, a thick baked omelette containing poached chicken and chestnuts with a light-golden crust on the top. I note down the ingredients and the method and, struck by the cornucopia of creativity, I tell Ruvinova that her dishes are "a culinary poem to all things Mountain Jewish." She laughs and then corrects me by saying, "yes, they are. But they are made all the better for also being a little bit Russian and a little bit Azeri too." Ethnic unity on a plate.

the synagogue at Gyrmyzy Gasaba, Azerbaijan

Mountain Jew Omelet

Serves 4

For the poached chicken

2 chicken legs

1 onion, coarsely chopped

1 carrot, coarsely chopped

1 celery stalk, coarsely chopped

2 bay leaves

1 teaspoon sea salt

1 teaspoon black peppercorns

For the khoyagusht

2 tablespoons butter

2 onions, sliced

1 teaspoon ground turmeric

1 teaspoon paprika

7 ounces cooked and peeled
  chestnuts, halved

4 eggs

sea salt and freshly
  ground black pepper

The Mountain Jews of Azerbaijan need hearty food to sustain them through bitter winters. Their culinary heritage draws much on Persian influence, and a staple dish is khoyagusht. Baked in a pan, the eggs puff up like an omelet, encasing the shreds of tender chicken below. It is usually served cut in wedges with rice, but any leftovers make a great filling wrapped in flatbread.

Put the chicken legs in a pan with all the aromatics and cover with cold water. Bring to a boil, cover the pan, and turn the heat down to simmer for 25 to 30 minutes until cooked through. Drain the chicken and reserve the broth. Remove the skin and bones, and shred the meat.

For the khoyagusht, heat a frying pan and add the butter and any fat from the top of the broth. Cook the onions until softened, then add a ladleful of the broth from the chicken. Continue cooking until the liquid has evaporated and the onions are light golden. Season with salt and pepper and add the turmeric and paprika.

Add the shredded chicken and the chestnuts to the pan, and stir everything together. Moisten with another small ladleful of the chicken broth. Cover with a lid and simmer for 10 minutes for the flavors to meld.

Preheat the broiler.

Lightly beat the eggs with salt and pepper. Pour over the top of the meat and use a spoon to make holes in the meat, encouraging the egg into the gaps. Put under the hot broiler just to set the eggs and slightly brown the top. (You may need to protect the handle of the pan.) Leave the khoyagusht to sit in the pan for 5 minutes before turning onto a plate and cutting into wedges to serve.

Georgian Chicken with Walnut Sauce

Serves 4

1 chicken (about 3¼ pounds)
1 teaspoon ground coriander
½ teaspoon cayenne pepper
½ teaspoon sea salt
2 tablespoons olive oil
½ lemon

For the walnut sauce
1 cup fresh cilantro leaves
½ cup walnuts
2 garlic cloves, crushed
1 teaspoon fenugreek seeds
½ teaspoon ground coriander
½ teaspoon ground turmeric
juice of ½ lemon
⅔ cup hot chicken stock
  or water
sea salt and freshly ground
  black pepper

Garo is an herby walnut sauce made with fenugreek seeds, which give it an unusual but intriguing flavor. This sauce is ubiquitous in Georgian cooking, served with meat, fish, vegetables, and even eggs. It works particularly well with roast chicken.

Preheat the oven to 375°F.

Season the chicken inside and out, and dust with the ground coriander and cayenne. Drizzle with the olive oil and use your hands to rub the oil and spices into the skin well. Squeeze over the lemon juice and place the squeezed-out skin into the cavity. Place the chicken in a roasting pan and roast for 1 hour 10 minutes, or until the juices run clear.

Meanwhile, make the sauce: Put all the ingredients, except the stock, into a food processor and process to a paste. Pour in the chicken stock with the motor running. Transfer to a pan and simmer for 10 minutes, stirring often. Remove from the heat, let cool to room temperature, and taste for seasoning.

Serve the chicken hot or cold with the walnut sauce.

Chicken, Potato, and Prune Hotpot

Serves 4

4 chicken legs
sea salt and freshly ground
  black pepper
3 tablespoons olive oil
1 pound waxy potatoes,
  unpeeled and cut into ¾-inch
  chunks
2 sweet apples, unpeeled,
  cored and cut into ¾-inch
  chunks
½ teaspoon allspice
2 tablespoons tomato paste
½ cup prunes, pitted and
  halved
⅓ cup dried apricots,
  quartered
2¾ hot cups chicken stock

To serve
a small bunch of tarragon
  leaves
3 tablespoons pistachios,
  chopped

Fruits paired with meat are a staple of Central Asia, lending both sweetness and tang. This is a cozy, one-pot dish, inspired by the flavors of the region.

Season the chicken legs with salt and pepper. Heat the oil in a saucepan large enough to accommodate the chicken in a single uncrowded layer and add the chicken legs. Brown well on both sides, then remove from the pan and set aside.

Add the potatoes and apples, and cook for 8 minutes over medium heat, stirring occasionally. Stir in the allspice, tomato paste, and dried fruits. Return the chicken legs to the pan, tucking them in among the potato and fruits.

Pour in the chicken stock and bring to a boil. Cover with a lid, turn down the heat, and simmer for 45 to 60 minutes, until the chicken is tender. Remove the lid for the final 10 minutes so the sauce reduces a little.

Serve sprinkled with the tarragon and pistachios.

Spicy Meatballs with Adjika and Yogurt

Serves 4

For the adjika

4 red chiles, seeded

4 tomatoes, seeded

4 garlic cloves, coarsely chopped

½ celery stalk, coarsely chopped

1 cup cilantro leaves

1 cup basil leaves

1 cup dill fronds

2 tablespoons walnut oil

2 tablespoons olive oil

3 tablespoons red wine vinegar

1 teaspoon sugar

1 teaspoon sea salt

For the meatballs

1 slice white bread, crusts removed

6 tablespoons milk

9 ounces ground pork

9 ounces ground beef

1 onion, finely chopped

2 garlic cloves, crushed

1 tablespoon barberries

1 tablespoon ground sumac

½ teaspoon cayenne pepper

½ teaspoon ground coriander

½ teaspoon ground black pepper

2 teaspoons sea salt

olive oil, for frying

Greek yogurt, to serve

Adjika, literally "red salt," is a spicy and fragrant pepper paste from Abkhazia, a breakaway region of Georgia. You'll find it completely addictive and you'll be using it as a condiment for everything, as they do in Abkhazia. It will keep in the fridge for a few days.

For the adjika, put all the ingredients into a food processor and pulse-blend to a chunky paste. The flavor will become more rounded and mellow if you make the paste in advance and let sit for a while.

To make the meatballs, soak the bread in the milk for about 10 minutes. Meanwhile, put all the other ingredients into a large bowl and use your hands to combine everything thoroughly. Mash together the bread and milk to make a paste, then mix this into the meatball mixture. Roll into meatballs; I like them golf-ball sized.

Heat a slick of oil in a frying pan and cook the meatballs in batches. Start at a high heat to brown the outside, then lower the temperature until the meat is cooked through.

Serve with the adjika and a generous dollop of yogurt.

A morning in Almaty's Green Bazaar

The Green Bazaar in Almaty, Kazakhstan's former capital, is the city's biggest market. A world away from the boutiques and neatly swept pavement cafés most visitors see, it is in a dust-choked and hard-up part of the city. This is where Hajj travel agencies jostle for space around the main mosque, with makeshift stalls selling everything from knock-off Adidas tracksuits to frilly knickers.

Inside the market, order reigns. On the ground floor, vendors wearing identical white catering hats preside over creaking turquoise scales, weighing out every imaginable foodstuff (including mandrake roots and unidentifiable herbs promising "long life").

Azeri men in their trademark heavy leather coats sell dried apricots, pistachios, and walnuts, while Korean women take orders for shredded carrot and fermented cauliflower, their hands spinning like atoms as they bag up the salads. On the upper floor, cafés do a brisk trade in plov and laghman.

Lines form at the wood-paneled counters selling kumis (fermented mare's milk) and shubat (fermented camel's milk), but I'm drawn to the multi-lane horsemeat section. The saying "Kazakhs are born on the horse" harks back to their nomadic ancestors, but today the connection between man and horse lives on in the cities as much as on the steppe. Knowing this, it was only a minor surprise to spot a "roulade of Kazakh horse leg in Caspian Red wine" on the menu at the western-style InterContinental hotel in Almaty.

Among piles of intestines, ribs, and rumps of horsemeat, I ask Aisha, a middle-class Kazakh, dressed in a white trouser suit and lemon-colored snakeskin shoes, about her horse-eating habits. She tells me that a small amount of horsemeat a day is essential for her family's wellbeing. Feeding her four children every day with horsemeat means they "get no flu, no illnesses at all," she says. Slapping a hunk on the scales, the vendor chips in "this is local meat, from just 30 miles away. It is full of goodness." It might be twice the cost of lamb, but for families like Aisha's, it seems a vitamin-packed horsemeat sausage a day keeps the doctor away.

Selling dried and fresh fruit and spices at Almaty's Green Bazaar

Azerbaijani Lamb with Chestnuts

Serves 4

3 tablespoons olive oil
1 braising lamb, cut into
  chunks
2 onions, chopped
1 teaspoon fennel seeds
1 teaspoon ground cinnamon
1 teaspoon Turkish red pepper
  or Aleppo pepper
½ teaspoon ground turmeric
3 tablespoons tomato paste
sea salt and freshly ground
  black pepper
1¼ cups pomegranate juice
¾ cup hot lamb or chicken
  stock
2 tablespoons pomegranate
  molasses
3½ ounces cooked and peeled
  chestnuts

To serve
fresh mint leaves
seeds of 1 pomegranate

This stew of melting lamb in an intriguing, sweet tangy sauce makes an excellent partner for the Buttered Rice Under a Shah's Crown (page 126).

Heat the oil in a large, heavy pan and brown the lamb in batches. Set the meat aside and add the onions to the pan to soften and caramelize, adding a little more oil if needed. Stir in the spices and tomato paste, then return the lamb to the pan and season with salt and pepper.

Pour in the pomegranate juice, stock, and pomegranate molasses. Bring to a boil, then turn down the heat, cover the pan, and simmer for 1½ hours, or until the meat is really tender.

Add the chestnuts and cook for another 10 minutes. Garnish with mint and pomegranate seeds, and serve.

Spring Lamb and New Potato Dimlama

Serves 4

3 tablespoons sunflower oil
2 onions, diced
1¼ pounds lamb neck, cubed
sea salt
3 garlic cloves, crushed
1 teaspoon cumin seeds
1 teaspoon coriander seeds, crushed
1 teaspoon cayenne pepper
1 teaspoon paprika
½ teaspoon ground black pepper
2 tablespoons tomato paste
1¼ cups hot lamb or chicken stock
1½ cups baby carrots or carrots, cut into batons
5½ ounces baby potatoes
a large bunch of watercress

Dimlama is a Uzbek stew in which meat and vegetables are cooked in layers, all intensifying in flavor as they simmer in their own juices. It is the Uzbeks' one-pot response to springtime, as fresh vegetables start to emerge after a long, cold winter.

Heat the oil in a large, heavy pan. Add the onion, and cook until softened, then add the lamb and season with salt. Cook, stirring occasionally, for about 10 minutes until the lamb is well-browned. Add the garlic, spices, and tomato paste, and cook for a minute longer.

Pour in the stock and bring to a boil. Turn down the heat, cover the pan, and simmer gently for 1 hour. Stir, and add a little more liquid if the sauce is looking dry. Scatter with the carrots in a layer on top of the meat, then add a layer of potatoes, halved if larger than a golf ball. Cover and simmer for another 30 minutes.

Check that the meat and vegetables are tender, then remove from the heat. Add the watercress in a final layer and cover with the lid. Let steam just long enough for the watercress to begin to wilt, perhaps 30 seconds, then serve.

Plovs & Pilafs

The undisputed king of Uzbek cuisine

Plov, a steaming pilaf that is cooked in layers, is served almost everywhere in Central Asia. Legend has it that it made its first appearance in the region when Alexander the Great ordered his cooks to create an easy but satisfying campaign meal for his soldiers. Today, there are literally thousands of variations throughout Central Asia and the Caucasus, but the Uzbeks are the self-proclaimed masters of plov. Across Uzbekistan, tables groan under the weight of huge lagans (ceramic plates) of plov.

At its most basic, plov is rice, onions, and carrots with either lamb or beef, but in reality it is much more than that. For Uzbeks, it represents hospitality, community, and identity. In cities, towns, and tiny villages, the air is laced with the aroma of carrots, meat, and rice that drifts up from bubbling cauldron-like *kazans*. Plov is a fittingly hearty dish for a country whose national sport is kurash, a form of upright wrestling.

Early travelers to Central Asia often returned home with lively tales of epic plov feasts. Explorer and professor of oriental languages, Arminius Vambery, wrote in his book *Travels in Central Asia in 1864*: "My pilgrim brethren always gave brilliant proofs of their bon ton. My only wonder is that they could support the heavy plov, for upon one occasion I reckoned that each of them had devoured one pound of fat from the tail of the sheep, two pounds of rice, without taking any account of bread, carrots, turnips, and radishes."

Today, plov is nearly always served to foreign guests, leaving some visitors with the impression that plov is Central Asian food. According to tradition, Uzbeks believe that in order to make the plov really sing, it should be cooked outdoors by a man. Chefs use a lot of intuition to tell when the plov is ready. They can smell the aromatic meat and feel the heat coming off the rice. During the Soviet era, women took over most of the cooking, but master plov chefs,

known as *oshpaz*, are often male. At weddings, birthday parties, and during holidays the most skilled *oshpaz* can serve hundreds of people from a single *kazan*. An *oshpaz* is recognized not only for his skills but also his wealth, for the grandest *kazan* can cost several month's wages.

In Samarkand—a city sometimes scented by plov—the dish is decorated with quail's eggs and is traditionally eaten on Tuesdays and Sundays. The *lagan* is placed in the middle of the table and the plov served in layers—first rice, then vegetables and finally, the meat. Cooked correctly, it is beautifully aromatic and melts in the mouth.

During annual festivals, special celebratory plovs are served. Standout plovs are served during Novruz, the Persian New Year. Novruz plov varies across different regions but it is particularly spectacular in Baku, Azerbaijan. After prayers and hand washing in rosewater, two versions of plov are brought to the table. One, Ashgara plov, is made with chestnuts, onions, lamb, caramelized quince, and golden raisins, while the other, Areshta plov, is made with saffron-flavored rice, Puy lentils, and topped with wafer-thin sheets of lavash bread. In typical hospitable fashion, doors to the house are left unlocked throughout the festival.

Top: Women preparing plov for a wedding celebration

Samarkand Plov

Serves 6

2 cups basmati rice, rinsed

1¼ pounds stew beef, diced

salt and freshly ground black
  pepper

⅔ cup clarified butter or
  sunflower oil

4 onions, cut into wedges

2 bay leaves

4 yellow and 2 orange carrots
  (or use 6 orange), cut into
  thick matchsticks

1 teaspoon cumin seeds

½ teaspoon ground black
  pepper

½ teaspoon cayenne pepper

½ teaspoon paprika

12 garlic cloves, unpeeled

12 hard-boiled quail's eggs,
  peeled

**The quintessential dish of Uzbekistan, with as
many variants as there are people who cook it.
This Samarkand version is a little lighter than most
traditional Uzbek plovs, where pools of lamb tail fat
provide the dominant flavor. It can be made with
lamb or beef, and is distinctive for being cooked
and served in layers.**

**Plov should be eaten from one large dish placed on
the table to share, each diner digging in their fork.
It is said people form mutual love from a communal
plate and the joy of eating plov.**

You'll need a good, heavy-bottomed pan with a tight-fitting lid to
make plov. In Uzbekistan, a cast-iron *kazan* is used; a large cast-
iron casserole makes the perfect substitute.

Put the rinsed rice into a large bowl of cold water to soak while
you start the recipe. Season the beef with salt and pepper.

Heat the clarified butter in the *kazan* until hot and foaming.
Brown the beef over medium–high heat, in batches if necessary,
then remove from the pan with a slotted spoon leaving the butter
behind. Lower the heat to medium and add the onions. Cook,
stirring occasionally, until softened and golden. Return the beef to
the pan with any collected juices, the bay leaves, and a small cupful
of water. Bring to a boil then turn the heat down very low, cover the
pan, and gently simmer for 1 hour until the meat is tender.

Spread over the carrot matchsticks, but don't stir as you want to
keep the layers separate. Scatter with the spices and cover and
cook for another 10 minutes.

Drain the rice and layer it on top of the carrots. Poke the whole
garlic cloves into the rice and flatten the top with the back of

a spoon. Season very generously with salt and slowly pour in enough boiling water to just cover the top of the rice. Increase the heat and leave the pan uncovered so that the water starts to boil away.

When the liquid has cooked off, make six holes in the rice using the handle of a wooden spoon to help the steam escape. Cover the pan and cook at a low simmer for 5 minutes. Turn off the heat without removing the lid and leave the dish to steam undisturbed for another 10 minutes. If the rice isn't cooked, add a splash more boiling water and cover again.

Serve the layers in reverse, first spooning the rice onto the platter, then the carrots, and finally the tender chunks of meat on the top. Circle the hard-boiled quail's eggs around the edge. A juicy tomato salad is the perfect accompaniment.

Rosh Hashanah Plov with Barberries, Pomegranate, and Quince

A festival in Central Asia demands a large gathering—and of course a large plov. While the previous recipe is for an everyday plov, it can be easily transformed to one that is celebratory, studded with fruits and spices. For Bukharan Jews, the autumn festival of Rosh Hashanah (the Jewish New Year) is a perfect occasion to use glorious quinces and pomegranate at the height of their season.

Choose either beef or cubed leg of lamb. Add 1 teaspoon of ground cumin and 1 teaspoon of ground allspice to the pan with the onions. When you return the meat to the pan, also add 2 quinces, cut into wedges and cored. Along with the rice, tuck in a couple of cinnamon sticks and scatter with ½ cup of dried barberries or currants. Cook as above, then serve with fresh pomegranate seeds rained over the top instead of the quail's eggs.

Dushanbe Pilaf

Serves 4

For the meatballs
4 eggs
1 tablespoon all-purpose flour
1 pound ground lamb
1 onion, very finely chopped
1 teaspoon sea salt
1 teaspoon cumin seeds
1 teaspoon ground coriander
½ teaspoon paprika
sunflower oil, for frying

For the pilaf
1½ cups basmati rice
⅓ cup clarified butter
2 onions, chopped
3 carrots, cut into matchsticks
1 teaspoon ground cumin
1 teaspoon paprika
2 teaspoons barberries
  or currants
sea salt
a handful of dill fronds,
  chopped

In Dushanbe, the capital of Tajikistan, the favorite pilaf is made with meatballs stuffed with boiled eggs. Like elongated scotch eggs with Central Asian flavors, these look fantastic sliced in half on top of the rice.

Soak the rice in a bowl of water while you make the meatballs.

Put the eggs in a pan of cold water and bring to a boil. Boil for 3 to 4 minutes, then cool in a bowl of ice-cold water. Carefully peel them. Dust the eggs with the flour.

Mix together the lamb, onion, salt, and spices with your hands until well-blended. Form into four oval-shaped patties and carefully wrap each around a boiled egg. Squeeze the meat at the top and bottom to give the meatballs a slightly tapered shape. Chill in the fridge for 30 minutes to firm up.

Heat the oil in a large frying pan and cook the meatballs until well-browned on all sides and just cooked through. Set aside.

To cook the pilaf you need a large pan, ideally cast iron, with a lid. Heat the clarified butter and cook the onions and carrots until softened. Add the spices and cook for 1 to 2 minutes longer until the aroma hits you. Add a small cup of cold water and the barberries.

Lay the meatballs on top of the vegetables and cover with the drained rice. Season with salt and pour in enough boiling water to just cover the top of the rice. Increase the heat and let the water start to boil away. Once the water has cooked off, use the handle of a wooden spoon to poke holes into the rice to help the steam escape. Turn the heat down to the lowest setting and cover the pan. Cook for 5 minutes, then remove from the heat and let steam for another 10 minutes until the rice is cooked.

To serve, mix the rice and vegetables together on a platter. Cut the meatballs into halves and lay on top. Finally, scatter the whole dish with fresh dill.

Pumpkin Stuffed with Jeweled Rice

Serves 4

1 pumpkin (about 2¼ pounds)
olive oil
2 teaspoons ground cinnamon
1 scant teaspoon ground
   cardamom
1 teaspoon dried chile flakes
½ cup dried barberries or
   unsweetened dried
   cranberries
2 tablespoons orange blossom
   water
generous pinch of saffron
   strands
½ cup sliced almonds
½ cup pistachios, chopped
1 orange
2 tablespoons sugar
⅔ cup dried sour cherries
½ cup basmati rice, rinsed
sea salt and freshly ground
   black pepper
4 tablespoons butter

This pumpkin is roasted with a filling of Persian-style rice, studded with jewel-like colors from the fruit and nuts. Bring the whole pumpkin to the table to serve and cut into wedges for each diner.

Preheat the oven to 425°F. Cut a lid off the pumpkin and reserve it. Scrape out the seeds and straggly strands and discard. Continue scooping out more of the flesh, leaving the shell about 1-inch thick (save the flesh for soup). Rub the inside of the pumpkin with a little olive oil and the cinnamon, cardamom, and dried chile. Season with salt and pepper. Roast for 30 minutes.

Meanwhile, put the barberries into a bowl of cold water and let soak for about 15 minutes, then drain. Put the orange blossom water into a small bowl and crumble in the saffron. Set aside. Toast the almonds and pistachios in a dry pan. Set aside.

Use a peeler to remove half the orange zest in strips. Slice these crosswise into thin slivers. Bring a small pan of water to a boil, drop in the orange zest, boil for 1 minute, then drain and refresh under cold running water (this removes the bitterness.) Return the pan to the heat and add the sugar and a generous splash of water. Heat to dissolve the sugar, then add the orange zest and cook the liquid down to a syrup. Remove from the heat and stir in the toasted nuts, barberries, and sour cherries. Set aside.

Partially cook the rice in fast-boiling water for 6 minutes. Drain. Stir the fruity nut mixture through the rice, then drizzle with the orange blossom water. Season well. Spoon the jeweled rice into the pumpkin, top with the butter, and place the lid back on top.

Tear off a piece of aluminum foil large enough to double wrap the pumpkin and lay out on a baking sheet. Sit the pumpkin on top, rub the skin with a little olive oil, and wrap the foil around it. Roast or another 30 to 60 minutes until the flesh is tender and a knife goes in easily (allow more roasting time if there is resistance to the knife). Let sit for 10 minutes before serving.

Bukharian Family-style Chicken and Rice

Serves 4

2 tablespoons sunflower oil
2 onions, chopped
3 carrots, coarsely grated
2 teaspoons sugar
2 skinless chicken breasts,
  cut into bite-sized pieces
sea salt
½ teaspoon paprika
1¼ cups basmati rice,
  rinsed
8 garlic cloves, unpeeled
1½ cups hot chicken stock
3 tablespoons butter
½ cup cashews

Rice dishes in Central Asia tend to be grand affairs cooked slowly for weekends, holidays, and weddings, but they don't have to be. This simple one-pot family dish is one for weeknights and its gently spiced flavor makes it ideal for children.

This lovely fluffy pile of chicken and rice uses only simple flavors, so use the best ingredients you can. Ideally, that means homemade chicken stock, good chicken, organic carrots, and decent basmati rice.

Heat the oil in a sauté pan over medium–high heat. Add the onions, carrots, and sugar, and cook until softened.

Layer the chicken on top of the vegetables, but don't stir as you want to keep distinct layers. Cook in the steam of the vegetables until the meat starts to turn white. Carefully turn the chicken to cook the other side and season generously with salt and the paprika.

Layer the rice evenly over the chicken and use the handle of a wooden spoon to poke eight holes into the rice. Tuck a clove of garlic into each hole, then pour over the chicken stock. It should come up ½-inch above the rice (add more boiling water if needed). Turn the heat down low and cover the pan with a lid or a tight-fitting layer of aluminum foil. Cook for 30 minutes, or until the liquid is absorbed and the rice is tender.

Meanwhile, heat the butter in a small frying pan and toast the cashews until lightly golden.

Serve the layers in reverse order, spooning first the rice, then the chicken, and finally the vegetables onto each plate. Scatter the nuts over the top.

Green-herbed Plov with Chickpeas

Serves 4

7 tablespoons butter

3 onions, sliced

1 fennel bulb, sliced, any fronds saved and added to the herbs

1 teaspoon paprika

½ teaspoon ground coriander

½ teaspoon ground cumin

½ teaspoon cayenne pepper

1 (14-ounce) can chickpeas, drained and rinsed

3 garlic cloves, coarsely chopped

½ cup black olives, pitted and coarsely chopped

10½ ounces spinach, washed

a large bunch of parsley, leaves only

a small bunch of cilantro, leaves only

a handful of celery leaves

a handful of dill fronds

1¾ cups basmati rice, rinsed

juice of 1 lemon

sea salt

Vegetarianism is still rather an alien concept in Central Asia and it is hard to find a plov without meat as its central component. However, in Bukhara they cook a springtime plov using lots of wonderful fresh greens, which lends itself to this meat-free adaptation. A layer of herbs and spinach steams in the middle of the pan, scenting the rice above. You can substitute any greens and herbs you like.

Heat the butter in a large heavy-bottomed casserole pan or Dutch oven and cook the onions and fennel until softened. Stir in the spices and cook for 1 minute longer. Scatter the chickpeas, garlic, and olives on top in a layer, without stirring, and add a small cupful of cold water.

Chop the spinach leaves along with half the herbs and layer these over the chickpeas. Press down with a spoon as the steam begins to wilt and collapse the greens. Flatten the greens into a layer and pour in the drained rice, smoothing the surface with the back of a spoon. Season generously with salt. Pour in enough boiling water to just cover the rice. Cook over high heat until the liquid has boiled off. Use the handle of a wooden spoon to poke a few holes into the rice to allow the steam to escape. Cover the pan with a lid or aluminum foil and turn off the heat. Let the rice steam for 20 minutes.

Chop the remaining herbs. Spoon the plov onto a serving dish, carefully mixing together the layers along with the extra herbs. Spritz with the lemon juice and taste for seasoning.

Buttered Rice under a Shah's Crown

Serves 6 to 8

2¼ cups cups basmati rice, rinsed

9 tablespoons butter

generous pinch of saffron strands

sea salt

2 to 3 large sheets soft lavash bread

¾ cup cooked and peeled chestnuts

½ cup raisins or golden raisins

½ cup dried apricots, quartered

This splendid plov is a favorite at celebrations in Azerbaijan. The dish is encased in a crisp crust of lavash. When broken at the table, a mound of steaming rice tumbles out and the shards of bread conjure the shape of a Shah's crown.

To make the crust you need soft lavash bread, a thin unleavened bread eaten in the lands that surround the Caspian Sea. You'll find it in Middle-Eastern shops, otherwise substitute with flour tortillas.

In a large sauceapan, blanch the rice for 8 minutes. Drain and spread out on a baking sheet to cool. Melt the butter and set aside a small amount to grease the pan and lavash. To the rest, add the saffron and a pinch of salt, and set aside.

To assemble the pilaf you need a cast-iron pan about 8-inches in diameter. (Or you could use a high-sided cake pan, but wrap the outside in aluminum foil to keep melted butter from seeping out in the oven.) Grease the pan generously with butter and lay in the lavash to line the bottom and sides with a generous overhand. Fill any gaps with small pieces of lavash and brush with butter as you go.

Spoon one third of the blanched rice into the lined pan and crumble over the chestnuts. Add another third of the rice, then a layer of raisins and apricots. Finish with the remaining rice. Make holes in the rice using the handle of a wooden spoon and spoon over the sunny yellow saffron butter. Cover the rice with a final layer of lavash, then fold in the overhanging lavash to cover the top. Brush with butter and cover the pan with a lid or foil.

Preheat the oven to 350°F. Cook, covered, for 1 hour until golden brown. Let rest for 10 minutes, then invert the crowned plov onto a serving dish. Crack a hole in the middle and cut the crust into six sections. The shards will fall away, giving the look of the Shah's crown.

Chicken and Almond Pilaf Pie

Serves 6 to 8

For the pie
1 whole chicken (about
  3¼ pounds)
1 carrot, coarsely chopped
1 celery stalk, coarsely
  chopped
3 large onions
10 tablespoons butter
¾ cup sliced almonds
1½ cups long-grain or basmati
  rice, rinsed
1 teaspoon ground cinnamon
½ teaspoon ground allspice
½ teaspoon freshly ground
  black pepper
3 tablespoons golden raisins
salt and freshly ground
  black pepper
6 sheets of filo dough

For the saffron yogurt
small pinch of saffron strands
1 cup Greek yogurt
3 tablespoons extra virgin
  olive oil
3 tablespoons lemon juice
1 garlic clove, crushed

This fragrant pilaf is veiled under flaky filo dough, making it the perfect prepare-ahead dish for guests. All it needs is a salad or some sautéed greens as an accompaniment.

First poach the chicken, which will also make a simple broth in which to cook the rice. Put the chicken in a large pan and add the carrot, celery, and one of the onions, quartered but unpeeled. Pour in just-boiled water to just cover the chicken. Simmer for 1 hour, remove the bird from the meat-infused liquid, and let cool. Shred the meat from the carcass and chill in the fridge until needed. Meanwhile, return the chicken bones to the pan and bring to a boil. Cook to reduce; you will need 2 cups of hot stock in which to cook the rice. Strain and skim off any fat from the top.

To prepare the pilaf, heat a large pan. Chop the remaining two onions and cook in 3 tablespoons of the butter until soft. Add the almonds and cook, stirring often, until lightly colored. Pour in the rice, spices, and raisins, and stir to coat everything in the fat. Add 2 cups of hot stock and a generous spoonful of salt. Cook, covered and undisturbed, for about 10 minutes until the liquid has been absorbed and the rice is just tender. Remove the lid and allow the rice to cool. Fork through the rice and taste for seasoning. Chill until needed.

Melt the remaining butter and lay out the filo sheets under a damp kitchen towel, only taking out one at a time as needed to keep the rest from drying out.

To assemble the pie, brush a 9-inch springform cake pan with melted butter. Carefully line with a sheet of the filo dough, leaving the edges hanging over the pan. Brush with butter and repeat with three more sheets of filo dough, building up the layers and rotating the pan so the ragged overhang is evenly spaced around the edge. Save two sheets for the top, cutting each in half to give you four squares.

Spoon the filling into the pie. Cover with four final sheets and butter layers, then fold in the overhanging dough and crinkle it up to create a loose, crumpled lid. Brush everything with melted butter. At this point you can chill the pie for a day before cooking.

When you are ready to cook the pie, preheat the oven to 350°F. Bake the pie on a baking sheet for 40 minutes until the top is flaky and golden. Let sit in the pan for 10 minutes before releasing the pie.

While the pie is cooking, make the saffron yogurt: Put the saffron in a small bowl and pour in ¼ cup of just-boiled water. Let infuse for 10 minutes, then stir in the remaining ingredients. Season with salt.

Serve the pie hot or warm with the saffron yogurt on the side.

Sesame and Nut Bulgur Pilaf

Serves 4

5 tablespoons butter
3 onions, thinly sliced
sea salt and freshly ground
  black pepper
½ teaspoon ground cinnamon
pinch of ground cloves
pinch of ground mace
1 bay leaf
1¾ cups bulgur wheat
2 cups hot vegetable or
  chicken stock
¼ cup sesame seeds
¾ cup sliced almonds

A good accompaniment to meat dishes, but also a satisfying main course in its own right if topped with braised vegetables. The Sweet and Sour Braised Carrots on page 137 make a good match.

Heat the butter in a large pan and cook the onions with a pinch of salt until soft and deeply golden. Stir in the spices, the bay leaf, and the bulgur wheat.

Pour in the vegetable stock, season, and bring to a boil. Cover the pan, lower the heat, and simmer gently for 10 minutes. Turn off the heat but leave the lid on for another 5 minutes for the bulgur to steam.

Meanwhile, toast first the sesame seeds then the almonds in a dry pan until lightly golden. Stir the toasted seeds and nuts through the pilaf and taste for seasoning.

Fish and Saffron Pilaf

Serves 4

1½ cups basmati rice

4 onions (1 halved and
  3 thinly sliced)

1 tablespoon black
  peppercorns, crushed

1 bay leaf

a small bunch of parsley

sea salt

14 ounces sturgeon, monkfish,
  or halibut fillets

¼ cup sesame oil

3 carrots, sliced into
  matchsticks

a small handful of dill fronds

1 teaspoon dill seeds

1 teaspoon ground black
  pepper

large pinch of saffron strands,
  soaked in 3 tablespoons
  warm water

½ cup sour cream

juice of 1 lemon

Peculiar to Western Turkmenistan is a pilaf made with fish rather than the meat ubiquitous throughout Central Asia. Sturgeon from the Caspian Sea is the usual choice, but another firm white fish such as monkfish or halibut makes a good substitute.

Put the rice in a large bowl to soak while you poach the fish.

Bring 4 cups of water to a boil in a large pan and add the halved onion, along with the peppercorns, bay leaf, and the stems from the parsley. Season well with salt and lower in the fish fillets. Cook at a very gentle simmer until just opaque through to the middle, up to 10 minutes depending on the thickness. Remove the fish with a slotted spoon and set aside. Strain and reserve the broth. You'll use the pan again later.

You need a second large cooking pot in which to cook the rice. Heat the sesame oil until almost smoking, then add the sliced onions and the carrots. Stir-fry until the vegetables start to soften. Pour in the drained rice and smooth down with the back of a spoon. Pour in enough of the fish broth to cover the top of the rice by about ½-inch and salt generously. Bring to a boil and cook over high heat until the broth has boiled off. Use the spoon handle to poke a few holes in the rice to help release the steam. Cover with a lid or tight-fitting layer of aluminum foil and remove from the heat. Let steam for 20 minutes for the rice to cook through.

Chop the parsley leaves and dill fronds, and add to the empty fish pan. Add the dill seeds, black pepper, the saffron and its soaking liquid, and season with salt. Stir in the sour cream and set over low heat to warm through. Carefully add the fish fillets to warm through in the saffron cream before serving.

Turn the rice onto a large platter and squeeze over the lemon. Spoon the fish and its creamy sauce on top.

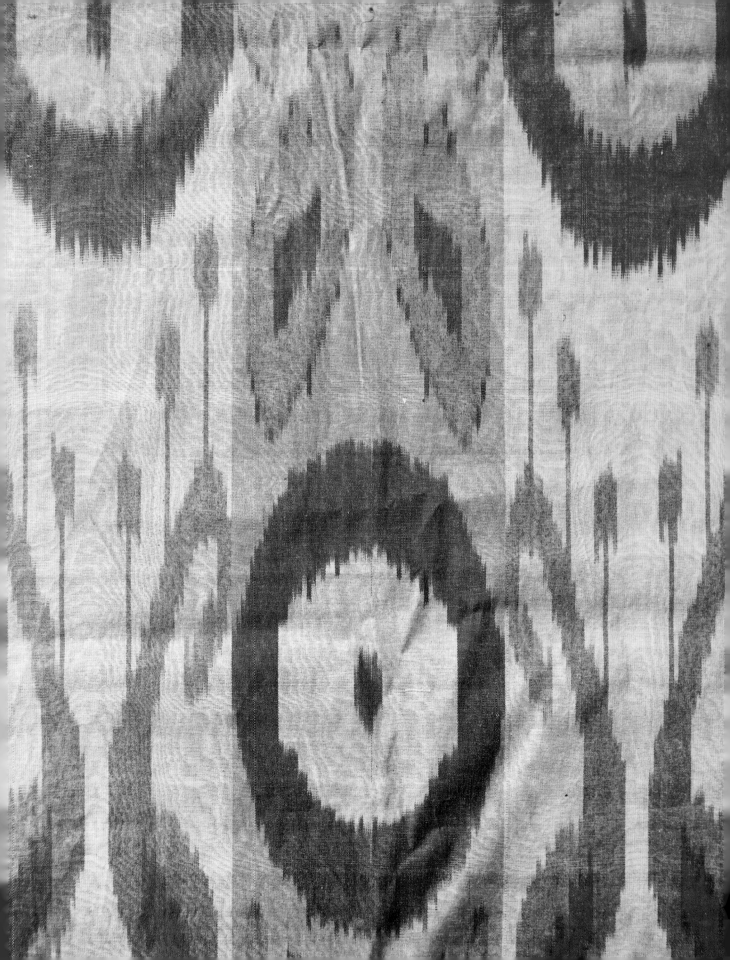

Accompaniments

Melting Potatoes with Dill

Serves 4

3 tablespoons butter

2 tablespoons olive oil

2 onions, sliced

1¼ pounds waxy potatoes, unpeeled and cut into ½-inch slices

3 garlic cloves, finely sliced

sea salt

1 teaspoon cracked black peppercorns

a small handful of dill fronds, chopped

Long, slow cooking in butter and only their own steam for liquid make these potatoes silky soft inside and caramelized on the outside.

Heat the butter and oil in a large frying pan and cook the onions very slowly until soft and golden. Add the potato slices and garlic, and stir to gloss them with the buttery onions. Season well with salt and cover with a lid or aluminum foil.

Leave the potatoes to cook over the lowest heat, stir occasionally, then replace the lid or foil, for about 45 minutes. Stir in the peppercorns and dill before serving.

Cinnamon Potatoes with Pine Nuts

Serves 4

1¼ pounds baby potatoes

3 tablespoons butter

1 onion, chopped

2 tablespoons pine nuts

2 teaspoons ground cinnamon

1 teaspoon ground coriander

1 teaspoon chile flakes

¼ teaspoon ground cardamom

1 teaspoon sugar

1 tablespoon pomegranate molasses

sea salt and freshly ground black pepper

This recipe from Azerbaijan has an unusual but very good combination of flavors.

First, evaluate your potatoes: Halve any that are larger than a golf ball. If they are thick-skinned, remove a strip around the center with a peeler to allow the flavors to penetrate. If the skins are thin, leave them intact.

Select a pan large enough to accommodate the potatoes in a single, snug-fitting layer. Melt the butter and sauté the onion and pine nuts until turning golden. Add the spices and cook for a minute, then stir in the potatoes. Add enough cold water to half cover the potatoes. Season with the sugar, pomegranate molasses, salt, and pepper. Cover and bring to a boil. When the water is simmering, turn the heat down and braise, turning the potatoes after about 10 minutes until just tender when pierced with the tip of a skewer. This should take about 20 minutes.

Remove the lid, increase the heat to high, and boil off the liquid, shaking the pan until the water evaporates and the butter begins to sizzle, caramelizing the onions and potatoes. Serve hot.

Jerusalem Artichokes with Rice, Parsley, and Tarragon

Serves 4

1¼ pounds Jerusalem artichokes
juice of 1 lemon
6 tablespoons extra virgin
 olive oil
4 shallots, finely chopped
⅓ cup rice, rinsed
sea salt and freshly ground
 black pepper
handful of parsley
handful of tarragon

What we call Jerusalem artichokes are known to the Turks as *yer elmasi*, literally "ground apples," and since Ottoman times they have been pickled, added to rice, and made into creamy soups. They are mainly farmed just outside the capital, Ankara, where fields of them are identifiable by their golden flowers in early fall.

Peel the Jerusalem artichokes then cut them into roughly 1¼-inch chunks. Drop them into a bowl of water with a little of the lemon juice—this keeps them from discoloring.

Heat the oil in a pan and add the shallots. Cook until softened and just starting to turn golden. At this point, drain the Jerusalem artichokes and add to the pan, stirring without adding liquid for a couple of minutes.

Add the rice, a good pinch of salt, and ½ cup of cold water. Bring to a boil, clamp on a well-fitting lid, and turn the heat down to low. Let cook undisturbed for 20 minutes, or until the rice and Jerusalem artichokes are tender.

Squeeze over the lemon juice and let cool to room temperature. Serve sprinkled with the parsley, tarragon, and lots of black pepper.

Sweet and Sour Braised Carrots

Serves 4

5 tablespoons butter
1 garlic clove, crushed
½ teaspoon ground cumin
½ teaspoon ground cinnamon
½ teaspoon chile flakes
2 tablespoons tomato paste
2 teaspoons sugar
juice of 1 lemon
14 ounces carrots (about
  5 large), cut into batons
1 tablespoon raisins
sea salt

Traditional Uzbek spicing, sweet raisins, and a tangy tomato glaze give a delicious and complex flavor to braised carrots.

Melt the butter in a pan. Add the garlic, cumin, cinnamon, and chile and cook, stirring, for 1 minute. Stir in the tomato paste, sugar, lemon juice, and a large pinch of salt.

Add the carrots and raisins to the pan along with ⅓ cup of cold water. Stir, bring to a boil, then turn the heat down and cover the pan. Cook, stirring occasionally, for 20 minutes, or until the carrots are tender.

Apricot and Orange Blossom Hosaf

Serves 4

¾ cup dried apricots, cut into
  quarters
¼ cup raisins or golden raisins
2 cloves
1 tablespoon sugar
1 tablespoon honey
1 tablespoon orange blossom
  water

Turkish people are adept at combining sweet and savory flavors. In sweet shops you can sample candied tomatoes, eggplants, and even olives. Hosaf is a sweet compote of dried fruits that is often paired with meaty pilafs.

Put all the ingredients in a small pan and add 1½ cups of water. Heat gently to melt the sugar and honey into a syrup, and simmer for 10 minutes to soften the fruit. Let cool and macerate for a few hours.

Discard the cloves and serve at room temperature.

Grape and Pistachio Orzo

Serves 4 to 6

1½ cups orzo pasta
sea salt and freshly ground
  black pepper
5 tablespoons olive oil
3 fat garlic cloves,
  finely chopped
juice of 1 lemon
½ cup nibbed pistachios
1½ cups seedless red grapes,
  halved
½ cup purple basil, sliced
  into ribbons

This clever pasta salad has found its way onto many online recipe blogs. It uses a flavor combination typical of Armenian cooking, where sweet fruits are married with savory flavors. You'll be amazed by the impact of the simple combination of grapes, pistachios, and basil.

Good Middle-Eastern stores will stock nibbed pistachios. The shape of these beautiful vibrant green shards perfectly complements that of the orzo, which resembles rice. If you can't find nibbed pistachios, soak shelled nuts for 10 minutes in just-boiled water, then rub off the skins. Dry the pistachios on a baking sheet in a very low oven for 10 minutes to regain their crunch. If you can forego the look but not the flavor, regular shelled pistachios will do too.

Cook the orzo pasta in salted boiling water according to the package instructions.

Meanwhile, warm the olive oil in a small frying pan and sizzle the garlic until cooked through and fragrant but not colored. Remove the pan from the heat and add the lemon juice, salt, and pepper.

Drain the orzo and immediately stir through the garlicky oil. Taste for seasoning. It can be chilled at this point until you are ready to serve (it's nicest brought back to room temperature if you do chill it) or you can continue and serve it warm.

Stir in the pistachios, grapes, and basil before serving, reserving a final scattering of each for the top.

Roasted Cauliflower with Pistachio and Tarragon

Serves 4

1 large cauliflower, broken into
  small florets
3 tablespoons olive oil
1 teaspoon cumin seeds
⅓ cup pistachios, toasted and
  lightly crushed
2 tablespoons chopped parsley
1 tablespoon sliced mint leaves
1 tablespoon torn tarragon
  leaves
seeds of ½ pomegranate
sea salt

Cauliflower wouldn't normally be served roasted in Uzbekistan, where oven cooking is done in commercial tandoors. However, the flavors of this dish give it an authentically Uzbek feel and roasting helps intensify the flavors.

Preheat the oven to 400°F. Toss the cauliflower with the olive oil and cumin seeds. Spread out in a single layer on a baking sheet and roast in the oven for 20 minutes, or until cooked through and golden brown.

Set aside to cool slightly before tossing with the remaining ingredients and a good pinch of salt.

Pumpkin with Uighur Seven Spice

Serves 4

For the seven spice
2 tablespoons cumin seeds
1½ tablespoons black
  peppercorns
1½ teaspoons Sichuan pepper
1½ teaspoons ground
  cinnamon
seeds of 3 green cardamom
  pods
2 cloves
2 star anise

2¼ pounds pumpkin or
  butternut squash, seeds and
  fibers discarded
3 tablespoons sunflower oil
½ teaspoon dried chile flakes
sea salt

The Uighurs are a Muslim minority group mainly residing in the far western corner of China. Just as the people—who are ethnically Turkic rather than Han Chinese—straddle two cultures, so does their food, which displays clear influences of both Central-Asian and Chinese flavors. I love their distinctive spice mix, combining earthy cumin and piquant Sichuan pepper. Uighur seven spice also makes a great rub for meat.

Roast the spices separately in a dry pan until fragrant. Grind together in a spice grinder or with a pestle and mortar.

Preheat the oven to 400°F. Cut the pumpkin into 2-inch chunks, leaving on the skin if you like. Toss with the oil, chile flakes, and a good pinch of the seven spice mixture. Season with salt and spread out on a baking sheet in a single layer. Roast for 30 to 40 minutes, turning half way through the cooking time, until golden brown and caramelized.

Going nuts on the Black Sea

Hulking ships waiting to carry everything from grain to furniture to the Caucasus and Russia lay like beached whales at the Black Sea port in Trabzon, or ancient Trebizond. Dating back to medieval times, the Turkish city I stand in today oozes the gritty atmosphere you can only find at port. Yet, despite the kebab shops, shady tea gardens (serving tea grown in Rize, just along the coast), and gray volcanic stone buildings, historic trading and maritime ties still dominate the scene.

It was from these shores that Marco Polo set sail to Constantinople on his return voyage from Asia in the late thirteenth century. Around the same time, following the Mongol conquest of Persia, Trebizond became an artery on the Silk Road. From Samarkand, and further east, Greek and Italian ships took merchandise to Constantinople and onward to the west. The Seljuks (the ancestors of Azeris, Turks, and Turkmen) had already set up caravanserais dotted across Turkey, providing accommodation for traveling merchants. Also around this time, Tamerlane, that fourteenth-century conqueror of nations, carried off to Samarkand master gunsmiths, silversmiths, and masons from Turkey. Legend has it that the craftsmen were personally plied with meat and coins by Tamerlane to spur them on.

Turning my back to the Black Sea, I look up at the etchings on the outer walls of the thirteenth-century Byzantine church of Hagia Sophia, a less glamorous sister to its famous namesake in Istanbul. During WWI it was used by the Russian military as a makeshift hospital but today, after restoration, the ancient graffito of galleons and ships etched on the outer walls, serves as a reminder of Turkey's seafaring and trading. It's said that sailors engraved these boats here to thank god for their safe arrival to shore. Inside, tiny chattering birds zip in through the windows as if to visit the golden tiers of angels that shine beatifically on the inner dome murals.

It is easy to get bogged down with Trabzon's long seafaring history, but there's another industry here that has long sustained this part of Turkey: hazelnuts.

Turkey produces 70 percent of the world's hazelnuts, and come late summer, they are hand-harvested all along the Black Sea coast. It's been like this for centuries. Ottoman chronicles record hazelnut tree landscapes and the wood has long been used to make everything from baskets to walking sticks. Even the local bus service is named after hazelnuts (*fındık*).

My first stop is Cirav Fındık, a shop that has been selling nuts since 1940. Inside, piles of blanched, roasted, sliced, shelled, and natural nuts (keeping part of the shell intact gives a more complex flavor) are being bagged up for hungry customers. I buy a jar of hazelnut paste that I'm told is very good for breakfast, "like a healthier Nutella," the shopkeeper jokes. I later discover that Black Sea hazelnuts actually do make it into jars of this globally popular spread.

The windows of nearby bakeries display rounds of hazelnut bread and cakes made from ground hazelnuts. At one, I stop and sink my teeth into a sticky super-sweet mound of kocaman gerdani (giant's nape) baklava, said to resemble the rolls of fat on the back of a chubby man's neck. It is a sticky mess of finger-licking delight with an added richness that comes from sun-dried hazelnuts.

It's not an exaggeration to say that the people of Trabzon are mad about nuts. A conservative part of Turkey where it's pretty tough to find a cold beer, when night falls here it's not "liquor" that neon signs flash above cafés, but "fındık": hazelnuts.

Green Beans with Hazelnut Tarator

Serves 4

1 ounce (about 1 slice) country
  bread, crust removed
⅓ cup blanched hazelnuts,
  plus extra to serve
1 garlic clove, crushed
juice of ½ lemon
3 tablespoons plain yogurt
¼ cup extra virgin olive oil,
  plus extra to serve
sea salt and freshly ground
  black pepper
1 pound 2 ounces green beans

Hazelnuts have been grown along Turkey's Black Sea coast for more than two thousand years, and today the country is the world's largest producer. Unsurprisingly, the nuts feature prominently in the Turkish kitchen. In this recipe they are transformed into a garlicky sauce called tarator, which makes a great accompaniment to seafood or vegetables. It is often paired with beets and their greens, but here gives a creamy coating to green beans.

Soak the bread in a bowl of water for a few minutes, then squeeze out as much of the water as possible. Put into a food processor with the hazelnuts and garlic, and process to a paste. Add the lemon juice, yogurt, and oil, and blend again. If needed, add cold water to thin the sauce to a smooth, dropping consistency. Season with salt and pepper.

Steam or boil the green beans until just tender. Drain and drizzle with the tarator and a little extra oil. Finish with a scattering of chopped hazelnuts.

Glazed Beets and Greens

Serves 4

4 medium beets with their
 green tops
2 tablespoons butter
1 red onion, thinly sliced
4 garlic cloves, flattened with
 a knife
3 tablespoons pomegranate
 molasses
1 tablespoon chopped tarragon
 leaves or dill fronds
sea salt and freshly ground
 black pepper

Beet greens are often overlooked in Western kitchens, but not so in Central Asia. If you have leaves left over from cooking the roots, stir-fry them quickly with garlic. This recipe makes use of the whole plant, coating everything in a tangy, buttery glaze.

Wash the beet greens and stems, coarsely chop, and set aside. Trim and peel the beets and cut each into four to six wedges, depending on their size.

Select a pan large enough to accommodate the beets in a single layer. Melt the butter, add the onion, and cook until softened, then add in the beet wedges and garlic. Drizzle with the pomegranate molasses and season with salt. Pour in enough cold water to almost cover the beets and bring to a boil. Cover with a lid, reduce the heat, and simmer for about 20 minutes, or until nearly tender.

Remove the lid, increase the heat, and boil off the liquid—you want tender beets coated in a syrupy glaze.

Scatter the greens over the beets, turn the heat down, and cover the pan. Cook for 5 minutes.

Uncover, add the tarragon or dill, and mix everything together in the pan. Taste for seasoning before serving.

Breads & Doughs

Baking Non Bread

It is lepyoshka to the Russians and çörek to the Turkmen, but to the Uzbeks and Tajiks, it is simply "non" (the word is Persian, but it is often transliterated as naan, and pronounced nahn). Right across Central Asia, these golden discs of bread are served at every meal along with steaming cups of chai.

Of all the peoples who bake non, from India, Pakistan, and Afghanistan to Central Asia and Iran, it is the Uzbeks who have turned this fabled bread into an art form. Generally, non is golden colored, the diameter of a dinner plate (but can come as small as a saucer or as big as a bicycle wheel) with a depressed center containing an indented pattern. A bit like a bagel, it is chewy, soft, and crisp all at once.

Throughout Uzbekistan different cities and provinces produce their own distinctive non. In Samarkand—where there are at least twenty different variations—it is heavy with a dark crust, while in the capital, Tashkent, it is lighter, softer, and less dense. In the ancient open-air museum-city of Khiva, non is noticeably thinner and crispier.

Differences aside, baking non follows a simple, time-honored sequence. The *nonvoy* (non baker) takes the dough, weighs it out, rolls it flat, stamps the bread with the decorative pattern, and then brushes the dough with an oil, egg, or milk wash, which adds a golden sheen. It is then sprinkled with onion seeds before being slapped onto the walls of a very hot clay tandoor oven.

Once always made at home, nowadays non is increasingly sold at bakeries and markets in Uzbekistan. At the break of day leagues of men load up their bicycles with non in preparation for their morning deliveries.

Special non utensils litter the markets and one of the best souvenirs to take home are *chekich*, the little tools with a hardwood handle and long metal teeth used to stamp floral or geometric patterns into the non. The reason for stamping the non is not solely decorative: chekich also release steam, which keeps the center of the bread from rising in the oven, keeping the middle crisp whereas the outer ring is soft and chewy. The more ornate stamps are brilliantly decorative and notable *nonvoys* have their own designs that they use as signatures.

Visitors to Central Asia need to know the special status of non. Here, if non is dropped on the floor, it must be placed in a place high up, like a window ledge, for beggars or birds. It is always torn by hand, never ever cut with a knife, and it is never placed patterned-side down. At weddings, the bride and groom both take a bite of a non at the ceremony and then finish it the next day as part of their first meal as man and wife. Family traditions also dictate that if a soldier goes off to war, he takes a bite of non as he departs and his family will hang the bread up and only take it down once he is safely home.

*Bread sellers
at the Siyob Bazaar,
Samarkand*

Non

Makes 1 loaf

1½ cups all-purpose flour
1½ teaspoons fast-action
 dried yeast
¾ teaspoon salt
½ teaspoon superfine sugar
sunflower oil or melted lard
½ teaspoon black onion seeds

Non is the flatbread that is made the length and breadth of Central Asia. It is usually baked by being slapped onto the searingly hot clay walls of a tandoor oven. At home, using a pizza stone and the oven cranked to maximum is the best way to achieve the characteristic chewy, elastic texture.

Put the flour in a large bowl, add the dried yeast to one side, and the salt and sugar to the other. Make a well in the center, pour in ½ cup of cold water, and mix thoroughly. If it feels stiff, add a little more water to make a sticky dough. Turn onto an oiled surface and knead for 10 minutes until the tackiness has gone and the dough is silky soft and smooth. Form into a ball and put in an oiled bowl. Cover with a kitchen towel and let rise for about 2 hours, or until at least doubled in size.

Knock the air out of the dough and form it into a domed round. Sit it on a floured wooden board lined with a piece of parchment paper and cover again with the kitchen towel. Let prove for another 45 minutes, or until doubled in size again.

Preheat the oven to 475°F, or as hot as it will go, and put a pizza stone or baking sheet in to heat up—it needs to get really hot before you bake the non.

Make an indentation in the middle of the bread by pressing with the heel of your hand, leaving a doughnut-shaped ring around the edge. Pierce a pattern in the middle using a non bread stamp or the tines of a fork. Brush the top with oil or lard and sprinkle with the onion seeds. Trim the excess parchment from the sides of the bread.

Put a handful of ice cubes on the bottom of the oven—this will create steam. Use the board to lift the bread to the oven and carefully slide it (still on the parchment paper) onto the preheated stone or pan. Bake for 15 minutes. The top should be golden and the loaf should sound hollow when tapped underneath.

A banquet on the Caspian Sea

"I learned the recipe of Azeri kebab, follow it and you will always be thankful to me for this present."
Alexandre Dumas

As night falls, Baku's audacious building projects light up. To my right is the newly built National Carpet Museum. Designed to look like a huge rolled up carpet, it glimmers against the navy-blue Caspian Sea, a land-locked ocean shared by five countries—Iran, Turkmenistan, Kazakhstan, Azerbaijan, and Russia. The museum is impressive but it is quickly outdone by Baku's Flame Towers. At twice the height of Big Ben, its curved sides flicker with 10,000 lights giving the impression of moving flames.

In the oil-funded neon glow that lines the boulevard, it's hard to imagine Azerbaijan's capital as an ancient city. But it is one. Baku can trace its roots back to the Egyptian's *Book of the Dead* and it has provided a vital link between the steppe lands and the West since Roman times. Buildings just a stone's throw from where I stand, in the more genteel Old Town, reveal Zoroastrian, Christian, and Islamic influences.

A ten-minute walk from the Caspian Sea puts me in the heart of this honey-colored cluster of observatories, bathhouses, and tiny mosques. Walking under rows of exquisite latticed hanging balconies, I trace the curve of the ancient ramparts, built in the twelfth century.

A string of vendors snooze in the dusk. In no rush for a sale, they barely look up as I stroke autumnal-colored rugs that paint manufacturers would describe as theater red and marigold. In Azerbaijan, these are not just for the floor, here they cover walls, sofas, chairs, beds, and tables. The thought of tables reminds me that one of Baku's best restaurants, Sumakh on Khojaly Avenue, is a short drive from the Old Town. I flag down a taxi.

The restaurant is full of families. Young women in vertiginous heels, obedient children, and patient fathers sit at tables laden with little plates of tempting morsels.

I start with a simple trio of salads: tomato and roasted eggplant, a plate of sheep cheese and a shepherd's salad of tiny scallions, dill, cilantro, purple basil, and cucumber. Next up is a plate of crescent-shaped *qutabs*—delicious flatbread pockets, stuffed with herbs and pumpkin, onto which I spoon sumac and dollops of sour cream. I then hungrily slurp a small bowl of *dograma*, a cold, refreshingly tart soup made from sour milk, potato, and cucumber. Black tea follows, served in tiny crystal glasses, alongside a platter of dried fruits and nuts—fat yellow raisins, dried unsulphured apricots, and pistachios, the kind that are sold by Azeri traders in many Central-Asian markets. My meal has perfectly expressed the strength of Azeri cuisine: its ingredients. Seasonal, full-flavored fruit and vegetables, naturally plump and sweet from the sun, speak for themselves. Every time I visit Baku I find myself wondering why more people don't know about this amazingly good food.

Top: The old town in Baku with the Flame Towers in the background; An open market in Baku, Azerbaijan

Uzbek Pumpkin Manti with Sour Tomato Sauce

Makes 20 to 24

For the dough
¾ cup all-purpose flour,
  plus extra for dusting
sea salt
1 egg

For the filling
2 tablespoons olive oil
1 small onion, finely chopped
9 ounces pumpkin or butternut
  squash, cut into ½-inch dice
¾ teaspoon soy sauce
¾ teaspoon honey
pinch of ground coriander
sea salt and freshly ground
  black pepper

For the sour tomato sauce
2 tablespoons olive oil
2 garlic cloves, crushed
1 (14-ounce) can chopped
  tomatoes
1 teaspoon paprika
1 tablespoon white wine
  vinegar
a handful of cilantro leaves,
  chopped

As trading routes crossed Central Asia, so an appetite for dumplings spread. Shapes and fillings vary widely, as do regional names. Variously called momo, aushak, tortellini, jiaozi, tabak, or, in Uzbekistan, where this recipe originates, manti. In summer, manti usually have a simply spiced meat filling, but in the fall it is more usual to use pumpkin right through until the swallows arrive in March, signaling the end of the pumpkin season.

For the dough, put the flour in a mixing bowl and add a pinch of salt. Make a well in the center and add the egg. Using your fingertips, gradually incorporate the flour. Bring together and knead for about 10 minutes until smooth, silky, and elastic rather than rough and floury. If it feels too stiff, wet your hands to introduce more liquid; if it feels too dry, add a little more flour. Wrap in plastic wrap and put in the fridge to rest for at least 30 minutes.

To make the filling, heat the olive oil in a lidded pan. Add the onion and cook until softened, then stir in the pumpkin. Cover with the lid and cook, stirring often, until the pumpkin is tender, adding a splash of cold water if it begins to stick. Stir in the soy sauce, honey, and coriander, and season with salt and pepper. Use a fork to coarsely mash the pumpkin and taste for seasoning.

For the sauce, heat the oil, add the garlic, and sizzle until barely colored before stirring in the tomatoes. Season with the paprika, vinegar, salt, and pepper. Simmer for 30 minutes, then stir in the cilantro.

To assemble the manti, flour the dough and work surface well. Use a pasta machine or rolling pin to roll the dough into a long thin strip about 2½-inches wide (setting 5 on a pasta machine). Cut into twenty 2½-inch squares. Put a spoonful of the filling onto each square and bring up the four corners . Pinch together the edges to create a seal—if your dough is dry a wet finger will help.

Bring a large pan of water to a boil. Lower in the manti and cook for 5 to 6 minutes, turning once during cooking. Drain and serve with the sour tomato sauce.

Khiva Egg Dumplings

Makes 8

1 quantity of dough
 (see page 156)
flour, for dusting

For the filling
3 eggs
1 tablespoon milk
sea salt and freshly ground
 black pepper

To serve
butter
Turkish red pepper or
 Aleppo pepper

These delicate dumplings are a bit difficult to cook as they need to be slipped into boiling water the moment they are made, but the effort is worth it. With a little practice, you should be able to set up a good production line and have more than one dumpling cooking at once.

Divide the dough into eight pieces, shape each into a ball, and lightly dust with flour. Use a pasta machine or rolling pin to roll each piece into a thin circle 4 inches in diameter. Put the rounds on a floured surface while you roll out the rest.

For the filling, beat the eggs with the milk in a spouted jug or container until smooth and season.

Ensure the dough is floured and not tacky. Make a paste by dipping a finger first in water, then in a little flour and run the paste around half of the edge of the dough, leaving a gap in the middle. Fold in half and crimp ½-inch around the edges together tightly, leaving a gap at the top. You want a semi-circular envelope with a small opening and a strong enough seal to contain the egg. Repeat with the remaining circles.

Bring a large pan of salted water to a boil. Make one dumpling at a time. Pour a little of the egg mixture into the opening, squeeze out any air, and seal up the gap. Immediately lower the dumpling into the water and cook for 3 minutes. Repeat with the rest. You'll be able to tell when they're ready as they'll float to the surface of the pan. Remove with a slotted spoon and toss with butter. Serve with a dusting of Turkish red pepper.

Dill, Cilantro, and Tarragon Flatbread

Makes 4

1¼ cups all-purpose flour, plus
  extra for dusting
sea salt
⅓ cup milk
a small handful of dill fronds
a small handful of cilantro
  leaves
a small handful of tarragon
  leaves
pinch of dill seeds (optional)
¾ cup hard cheese such as
  Cheddar, grated

To serve
melted butter
ground sumac

Qutab is one of the most popular Azeri foods. It is essentially a flatbread sandwich, filled while the dough is still raw, then cooked on a griddle, or saj. Our favorite has a simple herb filling. Dill seeds, if you can find them, is what Azeris like to use. Similar to caraway seeds; they bring another anise note along with the fresh dill and tarragon. The cheese adds a nice salty edge and gooeyness that's irresistible. Leave it out if you prefer.

For an entirely different filling, try spiced ground lamb with sour fruit paste (which you can buy or make by soaking fruit leather, as in the recipe on page 219) or a slick of fruit molasses.

Put the flour into a large bowl with a pinch of salt and make a well in the center. Pour in the milk while you mix with your other hand. Bring the dough together and knead for a good couple of minutes. You want it to be soft and pliable—if it is too dry, add a splash more milk; if it is too sticky, add a little more flour. If you have the time, wrap in plastic wrap and set aside to rest for 30 minutes as this will help you roll the dough out thinner.

Divide the dough into four equal pieces. Roll out each piece to a paper-thin round on a floured surface. It will take a bit of patience and elbow grease to get them really thin. Scatter a quarter of the herbs, dill seed, and cheese over one half, leaving a border all around. Run a wet finger around this border, then fold over the dough and press the edges together to lightly seal. Trim the edges into a neat half-moon.

Heat a large, dry frying pan or griddle over high heat. Cook the flatbreads, two at a time if they fit side by side, until blistered and golden on the bottom. Flip and cook on the other side, pressing down with a spatula as they puff up. Serve brushed generously with melted butter and dusted with a little sumac.

Kyrgyz Swirled Onion Flatbread

Makes 4

3 tablespoons butter
2 small onions, finely sliced
sea salt
pinch of chile powder (optional)
1½ cups all-purpose flour, plus
  extra for dusting
½ cup warm water
sunflower oil, for cooking

Flaky fried breads are popular in Kyrgyzstan, where they are served hot from the pan alongside soup. These flatbreads, called katama, can be made with or without yeast in the dough, but the sweet and slightly spicy caramelized onion is essential.

Heat the butter in a small heavy-bottomed frying pan over medium heat. Cook the onions with a pinch of salt, stirring often, until very soft and golden brown. Season with the chile powder (if using) and set aside to cool.

Put the flour in a large bowl with ½ teaspoon of salt and make a well in the center. Squeeze the onions using the back of a spoon and add any butter that comes out to the flour. Start trickling the warm water into the well while you mix with your other hand. Bring the dough together and knead for a good couple of minutes. You want dough that is soft and pliable—if it is too dry, add a splash of water; if it is too sticky, add a little more flour.

Divide the dough into four equal pieces. Roll out each piece thinly on a floured surface and spread a quarter of the onion over the surface. Roll up into a tube, pinch the ends, and form the tube into a coil with the outside end tucked underneath. It should resemble a cinnamon roll. Finally, roll it flat again into cardboard-thin rounds. Repeat with the remaining dough. The rounds will contract as they sit so you'll need to pull them out a little flatter with your hands as you put them in the pan.

Heat a frying pan over medium–high heat and use paper towels to rub it with a little oil. Cook the breads for about 2 minutes on each side, turning after each minute. They should puff up a little and begin to blister as they cook. Serve hot from the pan.

Feasting in downtown Tbilisi

Strolling down a tree-lined street in Georgia's capital Tbilisi, I stop in front of an unassuming produce market. As I root through piles of apples, tomatoes, and peaches, I spot dozens of long, knobbly marigold-colored oddities hanging from above. Could they be candles? Dried sausages, perhaps? They don't look or smell like either. Edging closer, I reach out a hand. This immediately brings the shopkeeper. She stops me, takes a silver pair of scissors and nips the string that the curiosity hangs from. Then she hands me my first churchkhela, a "delicacy," she says.

Churchkhela is made from nuts dipped into a mixture of concentrated grape juice, flour, and sugar known as *tatara*. It is made in the fall when the grapes and nuts such as almonds, walnuts, and hazelnuts are harvested. I bite through the waxy dried grape juice coating and experience a myriad of flavors and nutty textures. The taste of raisins, mulberries, and an intense flavor of amaretto from the almonds whisks me out of the Caucasus straight to Samarkand. There, at the Siob Bazaar in the shadow of the Bibi-Khanym mosque, I remember tasting for the first time fat, chewy manuka raisins from the Central Asian highlands. Succulent, sun-soaked, and candy-like, they are heavenly, just like the ones densely packed into this churchkhela.

It is all connected. Tbilisi was once a post on the Silk Road, albeit a minor one, and it benefited from the traders that passed through. Marco Polo noted in his thirteenth-century travelogue the luxuries found in Georgia: "they have a great abundance of silk, and make cloths of silk and gold, the finest ever seen by man."

Today, Tbilisi has a captivating faded elegance. Along the main street, Rustaveli Avenue, neoclassical museums flank Orthodox churches and stark Soviet-style state offices. In the old town, spread along the west bank of the Mtkavari river, ornate latticed wooden balconies hang precariously over cobblestoned streets that lead to secret courtyards. There are curious beehive-shaped semi-subterranean sulphur bathhouses too, but the finest public bath of all is above ground, the Orbelinani, its ornate facades like the madrasas of Samarkand covered in tiles and mosaics that shimmer with turquoise and the deep cobalt blue glaze found on Chinese vasework. People have used the sulphurous water from these hot springs (*tbili* means "warm" in Georgian) since at least the fifth century. From the plaque outside the entrance I read that Alexander Pushkin bathed here, but it was the food in Tbilisi he was most taken with: "every Georgian dish is a poem" he mused. How right he was.

Food is hard-wired into Georgian culture and well-fed locals file in and out of avant-garde restaurants with Belle Époque-inspired interiors, creaky wooden staircases, and dusty, rug-strewn floors. I'm in one such place, and I'm about to become acquainted with a typical dinner, Tbilisi-style.

First to the table is a platter of sour sulguni cheese made from cow or goat milk, which has a layered texture similar to mozzarella, accompanied by spicy salsa-like adjika, a plate of pickled chiles and a pile of wafer-thin lavash bread. Then, a ketsi (clay) bowl of spinach pkhali (a minced vegetable dip) paired with a larger one of walnut-stuffed eggplant rolls appears. Concurrently, we are served a rousing bottle of amber-colored rkatsiteli from the local Pheasant's Tears winery—where wines are still fermented and aged in earthenware kvevri vessels. It is drunk with a heartfelt toast, then it's straight onto the trout tartare.

There is a pause before the ultimate Georgian comfort food, Adjarian khachapuri, arrives. This is one of Georgia's most famous dishes—a glistening canoe-shaped bread containing a wobbling, almost raw egg that has been lightly poached by a pool of oozing molten cheese. All around, big boisterous tables are kept amused by their nominated tamada (toastmaster) who

A greengrocer selling churchkhela in Tbilisi, Georgia

between courses erupts with one poetic toast after the other. These go out to fellow diners, the chef, ancestors, the newly born, and the long departed. If it is a serious event—an anniversary or birthday—the tamada has an assistant, the *alaverdi*, whose job it is to expound upon the toast.

As another cork is eased from a bottle, it's on to a large terracotta plate of beef that has been sautéed overnight in Saperavi, a deep red wine made from Georgia's native grape, turning the meat the color of baked cherry. Finally, after many hours, the feast concludes with a glass of *chacha* (local brandy) a perfect digestif after all that food.

Throughout the evening the lack of tourists left me with the distinct—albeit slightly misguided—feeling that I was discovering all this myself. On the walk back to my homestay, fit to burst, I was already making plans for a return visit.

Left: Shop window, selling fruits; Right: narrow streets of the old town, Tbilisi, Georgia

Spinach Khachapuri

Makes 2

For the dough
1¼ cups bread flour, plus
  extra for dusting
1 teaspoon fast-action
  dried yeast
½ teaspoon salt
¼ teaspoon superfine sugar
⅓ cup plain yogurt
2 tablespoons warm water

For the filling
2½ cups spinach leaves
1 cup firm mozzarella cheese,
  grated
½ cup feta cheese, crumbled
¼ cup ricotta cheese
2 scallions
1 tablespoon finely chopped
  flat-leaf parsley leaves
1 tablespoon finely chopped
  cilantro leaves
1 teaspoon chopped dill fronds
  or tarragon
3 eggs
salt and freshly ground black
  pepper

cold butter, to serve

Khachapuri, a hot cheese-filled bread, claims the title of Georgia's ultimate comfort food. It is so much a staple of the Georgian diet that the Khachapuri Index uses the price of the ingredients as a measure of local inflation.

Of the many variations, the most ubiquitous is the round, pizza-like imeritian. Families will have a large loaf to tear and share at the table, while street vendors make individual "beggar's purses." This recipe draws on different local traditions: plentiful fresh greens to cut the oiliness of the cheese, and the beautiful boat shape of the version made in Ajara on the Black Sea.

For the dough; sift the flour into a bowl, adding the yeast on one side and the salt and sugar on the other. Stir in the yogurt and water while you mix with your other hand. You may need a splash more warm water to bring the dough together, but it shouldn't be wet. Turn onto a floured surface and knead for about 10 minutes, until soft and silky. Return to the bowl, cover with a kitchen towel, and let rise for 2 hours.

For the filling, steam the spinach for 3 minutes, or until just wilted. Set aside to cool, then squeeze out all the liquid. Chop and put in a bowl with the cheeses, scallions, herbs, and one of the eggs. Mix well and season with salt and pepper.

Flour a rolling pin and work surface. Divide the dough in half, form each into a ball, then coax into a thin oval shape about 10 inches long with the rolling pin. Spoon the filling in mounds in the middle. Bring up the edges over the cheese and pinch together at the ends to create the hull of your boat shape.

Preheat the oven to 475°F and put a pizza stone or baking sheet in to get very hot. Using a floured cutting board, slide the khachapuri boats onto the hot stone. Bake for 12 to 15 minutes—the cheese should be puffed up and golden. Use a metal spoon to push aside the filling and create a well in the center. Break an egg into each boat and return to the oven for 5 minutes or until the egg is just set. Serve at once with a slice of cold butter on top.

Samsa

1 small onion, roughly chopped

7 ounces ground lamb

½ teaspoon ground cumin

½ teaspoon sea salt

¼ teaspoon freshly ground
  black pepper

1 (11-ounce) pack of puff pastry

1 medium egg, beaten

1 teaspoon black sesame seeds

These meaty Uzbek pastries share an etymological and culinary heritage with Indian samosas. Cooked on the walls of portable tandoor ovens in bustling market squares, you can buy them to eat hot with your fingers.

Put the onion in a food processor and pulse until very finely chopped. Add the ground lamb, cumin, salt, and pepper, and pulse again to bring the mixture together.

Roll out the pasty to a rectangle 10 x 12 inches and use a 3-inch cutter to stamp out 12 rounds. Drop a spoonful of the meat mixture onto each round, then bring up three sides and pinch together well to make a triangle. Repeat with the remaining dough.

Put the triangles seam-side down on a baking sheet. Brush the dough with beaten egg and sprinkle with the black sesame seeds. Chill until ready to cook.

Preheat the oven to 425°F.

Bake for 20 minutes until the dough is golden and the filling cooked through.

Drinks

Tarragon Soda

Serves 2

a small bunch of tarragon
1 tablespoon superfine sugar
juice of 3 limes
crushed ice
soda water

Bottles of the soft drink Tarhun (named after the Georgian word for tarragon) are on sale all over the Caucasus, Russia, and Kazakhstan. Recognizable by its lurid green color—and tarragon leaves on the label—it has a strong licorice kick. This homemade version is far more subtle in sweetness, color, and flavor, and is an altogether healthier and very refreshing alternative.

Muddle the tarragon and sugar together in a small jug using the end of a rolling pin (crushing the leaves releases their flavor). Stir in the lime juice, then top off with crushed ice and soda water.

Feeling racy? Add more sugar and top off with iced vodka instead of soda water.

Fabulously fermented

Second in importance only to bread, it is difficult to exaggerate the love that most Russians and Central Asians have for dairy products. Fermented milk drinks, butter, suzma, (a tart yogurt cheese, see the recipe on page 40), curds, and sour cream are considered healthy, feel-good foods packed full of calcium and protein. Consumed daily by most people across the entire region, dairy products cut through oily food, aid digestion, and cleanse the palate.

Generally, the landscape and seasons guide the plate. Nomads on the steppe who keep sheep and goats have a diet that mainly consists of milk products and meat. In the summer, mare's milk (kumis) is prepared in a smoked sheepskin flask, giving it a distinctive ripe milky flavor, while in the winter, rock-hard, air-dried cheese balls (qurut) are easy to transport and can be rehydrated and mixed with water for a vitamin hit during the bitter cold months.

In Azerbaijan, cold soups like dovga, a plain yogurt soup flavored with coriander and dill, is wonderfully freshening in the summer months, then, come winter, it is braced with lamb meatballs. In Turkey, ayran (see page 187), a salty, yogurt water mix not unlike Indian lassi, quenches the thirst on hot summer afternoons. Cacik—a yogurt and cucumber dip similar to cooling Indian raita—cuts through the richness of Turkish kebabs and is often eaten with lavash bread in Azerbaijan. Shubat, the summer sour-milk drink of the Kazakhs and Turkmen, is fermented camel's milk. Excitingly experimental for visitors to try, this tangy milk is traditionally served from wooden bowls. I heard one traveler describe it as "milk fizz."

Some of these dairy products come with added health benefits. In the Caucasus Mountains, many people who live to a grand old age—100 years and over—attribute their longevity to kefir, a yogurt-like drink. The slightly fizzy live cultures found in kefir boost the immune system and vitamin B levels. Kefir can be drunk as is, ladled into soups, or added to batter to make pancakes with a tangy bite.

Russia produces some of the very best dairy products in the world. Spoonfuls of smetana (sour cream) are added to almost everything and tvorog (a curdled soured milk that is hung in muslin to strain) is ubiquitous. If one saying sums up the importance of dairy in these parts it is the Russian adage *krov's molokom* (literally, "blood's milk") which means to look rosy-cheeked and full of life.

Left: Making suzma (a tart yogurt cheese)

Rye Bread Kvas

Makes 4 cups

5 slices (around 5½ ounces total) dark rye bread
2 tablespoons raisins
1 teaspoon caraway seeds, toasted
2 tablespoons honey
1 teaspoon fast-action dried yeast

Ever more buzz surrounds the health benefits of fermented foods. This barely alcoholic Russian drink is an easy and fun step into the world of fermenting, using just a few ingredients and requiring no special equipment.

Caramel notes come from the rye, raisins, and honey, but kvas is refreshing and a little bitter rather than sweet. Kvas is said to be one of the world's oldest drinks still popular today. Throughout the former Soviet Union, the emergence of roadside sellers with their distinctive yellow metal kegs is a sure mark of the start of summer.

Day 1: Toast the rye bread until very well browned—darker color gives better flavor.

Bring 6 cups of water to a boil. Remove from the heat and stir in the toasted bread, raisins, and caraway seeds. Cover with a lid and let steep at room temperature overnight.

Day 2: In the morning, pass the liquid through a fine-mesh sieve into a clean pan, leaving the liquid to drip through the bready remains for about 1 hour, rather than squeezing it out. Discard the bread.

Heat the infused liquid until it comes to body temperature, then remove from the heat and stir in the honey and yeast. Cover again and let ferment in a warm room until the end of the day, by which time a good foamy head should have formed on the surface.

Skim off the foam and decant the liquid into a 1.5-quart plastic bottle. Add a few raisins to the bottle and seal. Chill in the fridge.

Day 3: The kvas is ready to drink. It is best served with lots of ice and with lemon or a sprig or mint. It will keep, refrigerated, for 1 week.

Infused Vodkas

A Soviet past has left a taste for vodka across the region. These are best served ice cold and neat to showcase the subtle perfumed flavors.

Cherry Vodka

Halve and pit 14 ounces of cherries. Put them into a large jar with ¾ cup of superfine sugar and a 750ml bottle of vodka. Shake well, then let infuse for anywhere between one and six months.

Saffron Orange Vodka

Add a generous pinch of saffron and two strips of orange zest to a 750ml bottle of vodka. Let infuse anywhere between one and six months.

Black and Pink Peppercorn Vodka

Add 1 tablespoon of whole black peppercorns and 1 tablespoon of whole pink peppercorns to a 750ml bottle of vodka. Let infuse anywhere between one week and one month. Taste every few days and strain once it has reached the pepperiness you like.

Rose Petal Vodka

Fill a large jar with organic rose petals (pinch off the white base to the petals first). Add ¾ cup of superfine sugar and 750ml vodka. Let infuse for two weeks, then strain.

Hot Honey and Lemon with Vodka

Serves 2

1 lemon
2 tablespoons honey
1 knob of ginger, peeled and sliced
1 cinnamon stick
2 shots of vodka

A Kyrgyz elixir to cure all ills.

Use a peeler to remove strips of zest from the lemon. Put the zest in a small pan with the honey, ginger, and cinnamon. Add 2 cups of cold water and bring to a simmer. Let infuse over low heat for 15 minutes, then strain into tea glasses.

Thinly slice the lemon and add a few slices to each glass, then splash in the vodka.

Vodka on the table, roses in the niche

In this part of the world, there are obvious challenges when it comes to syncing seven decades of atheist communist rule with the return of Islamic traditions. One of the biggest contradictions is alcohol. Russians introduced vodka to Central Asia and, for better or worse, an intoxicating stream of it has flowed freely into every corner of society ever since. Men file into little shops in remote parts of Central Asia to top off their vodka levels as you might a phone card, while countryside picnickers knock it back with abandon. In the cities, vodka accompanies dinners in posh restaurants and in shabby canteens alike.

Other more genteel traditions from Russia remain too—like Gardner porcelain. These cups, saucers, and teapots are instantly recognizable by their color—either oxblood red or sky blue—and their rose motifs. Made in Russia, they first began to circulate in the region in the mid-nineteenth century and can still be found today all over Central Asia.

It all began in the eighteenth century when an Englishman took advantage of Peter the Great's call for craftspeople to settle in Russia. In 1767, Francis Gardner opened his own, privately funded, factory close to Moscow. He produced porcelain dinner services in the floral Russian style of the time using roses as his trademark. Catherine the Great loved Gardner's craftsmanship so much that she ordered her own service for use in the Winter Palace.

Later, Gardner widened his market, selling to the Emirate of Bukhara and the Ottoman Empire. As Russia expanded into Central Asia, so did the Gardner style. Soon bazaars were full of mass-produced Gardner teapots and bowls, with some transported vast distances by horse and camel to cities such as Kabul and Khiva, to be handed down through generations as heirlooms. These bowls, teapots, and cups were often displayed in niches on walls, but were equally used in homes and chaikhanas. Some were manufactured large enough to be used as platters for plov, while more delicate items were encased in leather to protect them on long nomadic journeys across the steppe.

Today, it is possible to dine, surrounded by Gardner porcelain, in the Uzbek city of Bukhara. Akhbar House has a dining hall with a wall of niches where the porcelain is displayed, along with the alms bowls of whirling dervishes and vintage Korans that have resurfaced after being hidden by Soviet censors. Here, you can eat your plov and shashlik on Gardner porcelain and chase it with a shot or two of vodka, too.

Left: Private porcelain collection, Bukhara, Uzbekistan

Rhubarb, Apple, and Clove Kompot

Makes 4 cups

⅔ cup superfine sugar,
  or to taste
3 rhubarb stalks, roughly
  chopped
1 apple, cored and coarsely
  chopped
4 cloves

To serve
crushed ice
lemon slices

Kompot is a clear, refreshing drink that can be made with any fruit—whatever needs using up. Cherries, berries, plums, and peaches are all popular choices for making kompot in Russia, the Caucasus, Tajikistan, and across Eastern Europe. Have fun experimenting with different combinations of fruit and spice. Here is one for fans of sweet, tart rhubarb. The fruit leftover after steeping could be used in a pie or eaten with yogurt.

Bring 4 cups of water to a boil and add the sugar. Stir until dissolved, then add the rhubarb, apple, and cloves. Cover and simmer for 10 minutes.

Remove from the heat, add the lemon slices, and let cool completely. Strain and taste for sweetness, adding more sugar if you wish. Serve well-chilled with ice and lemon.

Apricot Sherbet

Makes 4 cups

2½ cups unsulphured dried
  apricots, chopped
½ cup superfine sugar

The word *sherbet* derives from the Arab *sharab*, a sweetened fruit drink that has barely changed in nature for over five centuries; Persian kings were said to drink theirs cooled with snow. Using dried apricots to make this simple Uzbek sherbet gives it a beautiful color and wonderful honeyed taste.

Put the apricots and sugar in a pan with 4 cups of water. Cover with a lid and simmer for 1 hour to infuse the flavors into the liquid. Let cool and sit for a few hours, then strain the liquid into a jug. Keep the poached apricots to eat with yogurt or in a pie.

Chill the sherbet well before serving over crushed ice.

Spice Route Teas

Inspired by teas I had at an old chaikana in Bukhara, these aromatic blends recall the days of the Silk Route traders. You can imagine them breaking their long travels in this desert city stop in Uzbekistan, enjoying pots of tea with sweets like the Pistachio Halva (see page 214) or the Sesame Brittle (see page 216).

Serves 4

Spices and Herbs Tea

Mix 1 teaspoon of dried oregano, ½ teaspoon of dried mint, 4 bruised cardamom pods, 2 cloves, ½ cinnamon stick, and 1 star anise, and put into a teapot with freshly boiled water. Brew for 5 minutes, then add 1 tablespoon of loose-leaf tea with bergamot (such as Earl Grey) and leave for another 2 minutes before straining into teacups or *piyala*.

Saffron Tea

Mix 8 bruised cardamom pods and a large pinch of saffron strands and put into a teapot with freshly boiled water. Brew for 5 minutes, then add 1 tablespoon of loose-leaf green tea and leave for another 2 minutes before straining into teacups or *piyala*.

Cumin Tea

Put 1 tablespoon of cumin seeds into a teapot with freshly boiled water. Brew for 5 minutes, then add 1 tablespoon of loose-leaf black tea and leave for another 2 minutes before straining into teacups or *piyala*.

Ginger Tea

Mix 1 thumb-size knob of peeled fresh ginger, chopped, 4 bruised cardamom pods, 2 cloves, and ½ cinnamon stick into a teapot with freshly boiled water. Brew for 5 minutes before straining into teacups or *piyala*.

Chaikanas & Samovars

From Kabul to Khiva the *chaikhana* (teahouse) in Central Asia is as much a meeting place for local men as the mosque. Every settlement throughout the region has both, just as the traditional English village once had a pub and church.

Tree-shaded and hushed, the chaikhana, all beautiful hand-painted ceilings, wood carved doors, and pillars, is where elders, known as *aksakal* (white beards), gather on *tapchans* (divans). Often doubling up as an informal courthouse and newsstand, this is where men (and it is always men) while away the hours putting the world to rights. Traders and travelers will arrive to refresh themselves, and while devouring smoky meaty kebabs known as shashlik and quenching their thirst with chai, they'll deliver tales of conflicts, and swap political opinions, and gossip.

In every chaikhana it is the *samovar* (literally "self-boiler") that rules the space. Representing hospitality, these metal urns stand ever ready for the thirsty male.

Samovars are simply designed. A central pipe burns hot, either with slow-burning coal or wood, boiling the water in the bottom urn, while the smaller top urn (*zavarka*) or teapot is filled with tea leaves and water. Once the leaves have brewed, the concentrated tea from the top is tempered with the hot plain water from the bottom urn, at a ratio of ten to one. In Central Asia, traditionally the tea is poured into a *piyala*—a special china cup without handles, similar to a Japanese *chawan*.

Just like the complex culinary histories of kebabs and pilaf or plov, the exact origin of the samovar is unknown. It is widely accepted that Genghis Khan's traders in the thirteenth century were the first to use samovars. However, in 1989, Azerbaijani archaeologist Tufan Akhundov unearthed a soot-covered samovar, thought to be 3,600 years old, in Sheki, in the foothills of the Caucasus Mountains. Whatever the samovar's birthplace, Tula, not far from Moscow, is the modern center of worldwide samovar production. One of the oldest centers of industry in Europe, known for its master gunmakers and blacksmiths, production of samovars in Tula started in the late eighteenth century. Popularity then increased production to the point that playwright Anton Chekov (tastelessly) quipped in his journal that "traveling to Paris with one's wife is as useless as traveling to Tula with your own samovar."

Today, most antique samovars that escaped being melted down for bullets on Stalin's orders during World War II, have found their way into museums and antique stores in New York and Moscow. You'll also come across *semavers* in the Black Sea region of Turkey. Turkey is one of the world's top producers of black tea called çay (chai) and in cities like Rize, in the eastern Black Sea region, there are plenty of semavers or caydanliks (two stacked kettles) being used to brew in the traditional way. The most coveted of Tula's samovars, created by master craftsmen such as Vasily Batashov, sometimes appear in the catalogs of top auction houses. Made of fine silver or copper, etched with ornate patterns, and complete with carved ivory or porcelain handles, these highly sought-after pieces cost enough to send an oligarch's credit card into meltdown.

Top: Man making tea wth a samovar in the village of Lahic, Azerbaijan; Bottom: Card game at a chaikhana, Uzbekistan

Armenian Herbal Teas

When the winter snows melt, the Armenian Highlands become carpeted with an abundance of wild flowers and herbs. Medieval manuscripts record herbal tea blends that have been made in these regions since ancient times.

Spiced Rose Petal Tea

For a two-person teapot, add 1 tablespoon of organic dried rose petals, ½ cinnamon stick, 2 whole cloves, and 3 bruised cardamom pods. Brew with freshly boiled water for 10 minutes.

Springtime Leaves Tea

To make this blend you need an equal quantity of dried hibiscus flowers, dried oregano, dried blackcurrant leaves, and dried nettles. Blackcurrant leaves can be found online or in specialty stores, and be sure to pick nettles before they flower, using gloves of course. Spread out the leaves on a rack and leave in a warm place for a day or two to dry out. Blend to a coarse powder in a food processor. Add 1 teaspoon of the springtime leaves blend per person when brewing a pot of tea and store the rest in an airtight jar.

Armenian Mountain Blend

For each person, brew 1 teaspoon of lime blossom and ½ teaspoon of dried thyme with freshly boiled water for 10 minutes.

Afghan Pink Chai

Serves 6

2 tablespoons loose-leaf
  green tea
6 green cardamom pods,
  bruised
1 cinnamon stick
1 star anise
¼ teaspoon baking soda
1 cup whole milk
2 to 4 tablespoons sugar,
  to taste
pinch of salt (optional)
¼ cup heavy cream, whipped

A tea made for special occasions in Afghanistan. It is served at the bride's house during weddings, while the groom's family will bring candies and pastries to enjoy with it.

With alchemic flare, green tea is first turned dark red through aeration and the addition of baking soda, then lightened to a dusky pink with the addition of milk and qymaq, which is similar to crème fraîche. The result is a rich and spiced flavor.

Bring 4 cups of water to a boil in a pan and add the green tea and spices. Cook for 5 to 10 minutes until the tea leaves have opened and turned the liquid green. Add the baking soda and boil for another 2 minutes.

Remove the pan from the heat and strain through a sieve into another pan. Continue to pour the tea from a height from one pan to another—this aerates the tea and turns it a deep red.

Return the tea to the heat and add the milk, clouding it to pink. Slowly heat to just below boiling point, then add sugar to taste (traditionally salt is added as well). Pour into small teacups and float 2 teaspoons of whipped heavy cream on top of each.

Ayran

Serves 1

⅓ glass Greek yogurt
⅓ glass soda water
pinch of salt
⅓ glass ice

A chilled yogurt drink most closely associated with Turkey, but enjoyed throughout Central Asia in the stifling summer months. It can be served plain or flavored with mint or black pepper. Try a glass alongside spicy kebabs (see pages 81 and 84).

Mix the yogurt, soda, and salt in a glass. Top off with ice.

Desserts & Sweetmeats

A Platter of Honey, Flatbread, and Dried Fruit

fresh figs, halved
grapes
mulberries
dried apricots
fresh yellow cherries or dried
  sour cherries
golden and black raisins
prunes
apricot kernels (find these
  in health-food or Middle-
  Eastern stores)
honeycomb
flatbread

As the fruits are so sweet in Central Asia, often no further dessert is needed. Instead, a typical meal will end with bowls of fresh or dried fruit, along with nuts and cup after cup of black or green chai, served in a small porcelain bowl, known as a *piyala*. These fruits and other treats will sit on the table throughout the meal for diners to dip into.

Choose a selection of seasonal fresh and dried fruit and assemble a generous platter. Add a wedge of good honeycomb and some warmed flatbreads to eat with it. Graze from the platter over the course of a long evening of drinking sweet tea and enjoying good company.

Roasted Peaches with Marzipan and Rose Syrup

Serves 6

3 ripe peaches, halved
  and pitted
¼ cup sugar
3 teaspoons rosewater
squeeze of lemon
½ cup ground almonds
¼ cup confectioners' sugar
2 teaspoons sliced almonds

Greek yogurt, to serve

Throughout the Caucasus, dried peaches stuffed with a sticky, sweet filling of walnut, almond, or pistachio marzipan are a popular street snack. Here, fresh peaches get the same treatment before being bathed in rose-scented syrup.

Preheat the oven to 350°F.

Snugly pack the peach halves, cut-side up, into an ovenproof dish.

Dissolve the sugar in 3 tablespoons of water over medium heat, then add 2 teaspoons of the rosewater. Taste, as rose concentrations vary hugely, so you may want to stop there or add a little more to make a subtly perfumed syrup. Sharpen with a squeeze of lemon and pour over the peaches.

Pulse the ground almonds, confectioners' sugar, and 1 teaspoon of rosewater in a food processor until the mixture comes together into a paste. Roll into six balls and stuff into each peach half. Scatter with the sliced almonds.

Roast for 30 minutes, or until the peaches are tender and slightly caramelized. If they are browning too fast, cover them with aluminum foil partway through cooking. Serve hot or at room temperature with thick Greek yogurt.

Sweet natured—the importance of mulberries

*"Now humble as the ripest mulberry
That will not hold the handling."*
Shakespeare, *The Tragedy of Coriolanus*

Central Asians and Turks share an almost obsessional love of mulberries. All across the region, the season for harvesting the fruit is eagerly awaited. When the time comes, bed sheets are held under mulberry trees and the trees shaken until a shower of berries rains down into the linen below.

In Turkey's Central Anatolia, the town of Aya hosts a popular annual mulberry festival. In Xinjiang, northwest China, home to the Uighur people, a Turkic ethnic group, mulberries from Kucha on the Silk Road are legendary, while a few hundred miles away in Hotan, another oasis city in this mountainous desert region, Uighurs make mulberry paper, a specialist art that has been carried out for 2,000 years. In Armenia, cold soups and salads are regularly sprinkled with mulberries, while in Azerbaijan men play nard (Persian backgammon) in the shade of mulberry trees, perhaps with a glass of *tut araghi*, a vodka-like spirit made from mulberry juice (in Armenia it's called *artsakh*). And everywhere when the fruit is ripe, birds fight noisily over the sweet berries, competing with children who shimmy up tree trunks to bag a share.

In the Uzbek cities of Samarkand, Tashkent, and Bukhara, the season for white mulberries is met with the sort of anticipation reserved for asparagus in Britain. For two weeks in May the fruit is sold first thing in markets because, by the afternoon, the delicate berries quickly spoil. This brings to mind the familiar nursery rhyme:

*Here we go round the mulberry bush,
The mulberry bush,
The mulberry bush.
Here we go round the mulberry bush
So early in the morning.*

White, red, or purple-red, ripe mulberries are super-rich in vitamins and antioxidants. In Tajikistan and Afghanistan, mulberries are boiled into a syrup which is then dried into sheets. Strips of this vitamin-laden sweet "leather" are carried by mountain villagers as a portable means of eating the succulent fruit to sustain them during the extreme winters.

Kefir Pancakes with Blackberry Syrup

Serves 2 to 4 (makes 12)

For the blackberry syrup
2 cups blackberries
¼ cup superfine sugar
juice of ½ lemon
pinch of allspice

For the pancakes
⅔ cup flour
½ teaspoon baking soda
2 teaspoons sugar
¼ teaspoon salt
1 egg
1 cup milk kefir or buttermilk
butter, for frying

To serve
fresh blackberries
sour cream

These Russian pancakes, popular across the former Soviet Union, are made fluffy and light by the fermented milk drink, kefir. They are delicious with any jam, or try this fresh blackberry syrup. And, of course, if you have mulberries, you could use those.

To make the blackberry syrup, put the blackberries and sugar in a pan (without any liquid). Heat, shaking occasionally, for a couple of minutes, just to break down the fruit. Add the lemon juice and allspice, and pass through a strainer.

To make the pancakes, sift the flour, baking soda, sugar, and salt into a bowl, and stir together. Make a well in the middle and add the egg and kefir. Use a whisk to incorporate the flour to make a smooth batter.

Heat a frying pan over medium heat and melt a small pat of butter. Ladle in the batter to make pancakes 3 to 4 inches across. Cook until bubbles rise to the surface and the underside is golden. Flip and cook the other side. Keep warm while you make the rest.

Serve hot with the blackberry syrup, a scattering of fresh blackberries, and spoonfuls of sour cream.

Apples are from Kazakhstan

Prince Ahmed's famous apple in *The Arabian Nights*—the one he thinks will win him the princess's hand in marriage—may well have been purchased in Samarkand, but to unearth the origins of this fruit requires a trip to Almaty, the former capital of Kazakhstan.

The Kazakhs' love of apples verges on the obsessional. Their market stalls overflow with them. In their kitchens, cooks have worked the fruit into well-known recipes: apples are braised with spices, sliced into Russian-style salads known as "herring in a fur coat" (potatoes, beets, herring, and lashings of mayonnaise), and added to plov. In Almaty, whose old name "Alma-Ata" means "fatherland of apples" in Kazakh, gnarly apple trees dominate gardens and every available roadside space. In the fall, a sweet smell wafts into town from the outskirts where countless fallen apples have created a cidery carpet.

A couple of hours' drive south of Almaty is Ile-Alatau National Park, sited on the northern slopes of the Tien Shan, the great mountain chain of Central Asia. There, where golden eagles soar, are tangled groves of Malus sieversii, the likely ancestors of almost all apples eaten today. Further east from Almaty, near the border with China, in the virgin forests of the Dzungarian Alps, thousands of acres of wild apples flourish, untouched by man. This is the only country in the world where apples grow wild as a forest.

The story of how the apple came to grow in Kazakhstan is simple: thousands of years ago a seed—an early forebear of the domestic apple—was transported by birds, probably from China, into the Tien Shan. There, safely billeted in the isolated mountain range, it quietly evolved into what became the apple as we know it today. Animals including brown bears and horses that browsed the mountain range got a taste for the fruit, swallowed the seeds, and spread them further afield, demonstrating early travel along the Silk Road at its most natural. Much later,

pastoral Kazakh nomads discovered the apples too, and carried them on horseback as a handy in-the-saddle snack, distributing their seeds further still.

Now, fast forward to the 1920s when botanist, seed collector, and plant breeder Nikolai Vavilov arrived in Almaty from Moscow on horseback. Troubled by crop failures and famine in his native Russia, he traveled to the Middle East, Afghanistan, North Africa and Ethiopia, collecting plants and devoting his life to the improvement of wheat and corn crops to alleviate human hunger.

He was impressed with what greeted him in Almaty: "All around the city one could see a vast expanse of wild apples covering the foothills which formed forests," he noted. His research confirmed Kazakhstan to be the birthplace of the apple, but in the 1930s Stalin denounced plant genetics. Vavilov was falsely accused of working for the American government and put in prison where, in the most terrible irony, he starved to death in 1943. Thankfully, in modern-day Russia, Vavilov is celebrated as a hero for his life's work.

Baklava Baked Apples

Serves 4

3 tablespoons butter, melted,
  plus extra for greasing
½ cup walnuts
½ teaspoon ground cinnamon
1 tablespoon lemon juice
3 tablespoons honey
3 tablespoons brown sugar
4 sheets of filo dough
2 tablespoons superfine sugar
4 tart apples, peeled and
  cored

Stuffed and baked apples are common in Central Asia, both sweet and savory. Here, I have filled them with the flavors from another favorite treat that evolved in the region—baklava. Sticky, scented nuts make the filling, while a shell of crisp pastry dough encases the fruit.

Preheat the oven to 375°F and butter an ovenproof dish.

Put the walnuts in a food processor and pulse blend to a coarse rubble. Stir in the cinnamon, lemon juice, honey, and brown sugar.

Work with one sheet of filo at a time, keeping the rest under a clean, damp kitchen towel. Brush a sheet of filo with melted butter and sprinkle with a teaspoon of the superfine sugar. Fold in half to make a square. Sit an apple in the middle of the dough and spoon one quarter of the filling into the core. Bring the four corners of dough up to wrap the apple well, brushing with melted butter as you go. Brush the surface with melted butter and another sprinkle of sugar. Put seam-side up into the baking dish and repeat with the remaining apples.

Bake for 25 to 30 minutes until the pastry shell is golden and the apple inside is tender. Serve warm.

Pumpkin Rice Pudding with Date Syrup

Serves 4

6 ounces pumpkin or
  butternut squash, peeled,
  seeds and fibers discarded,
  grated
½ cup medium-grain rice
2½ cups full-fat milk
1 teaspoon ground cinnamon
½ teaspoon ground nutmeg
½ teaspoon ground cardamom
½ teaspoon ground clove
2 tablespoons butter
date syrup (optional), plus
  extra to serve
sour cream, to serve

Rice pudding is universally popular and almost every country in the world has a version. Central Asia has its own array to add to the mix. A pistachio and cardamom-spiked pudding in which the rice is ground smooth is eaten in lands spanning from Tajikistan to India, while Persian influence brings rice and milk puddings perfumed with rosewater. During the sacred month of Muharram, a vivid yellow, saffron-stained rice pudding is made in Afghanistan.

Pumpkin brings an earthy sweetness to this dish, which is sometimes eaten for breakfast in Uzbekistan. Inspired by spice route flavors, I've added warming spices to make a comforting dish especially popular with children. Date syrup is a natural sweetener with a molasses depth. Taste before stirring any into the pudding, though, as the pumpkin may be sweet enough and you don't want to overwhelm the subtle flavors with sweetness. You can always drizzle with more syrup in the bowls.

Put the pumpkin, rice, milk, and spices in a deep pan. Stir well and bring to a boil. Lower the heat and gently simmer for 30 minutes, stirring occasionally, until the liquid is absorbed and the rice is cooked.

Stir in the butter and taste for sweetness. Add date syrup to taste (if using) and serve with another drizzle of syrup over the top, and perhaps a spoonful of sour cream.

Yogurt with Honeyed Walnuts and Turkish Cotton Candy

Serves 4

1 cup walnuts, coarsely
 chopped
2 tablespoons honey,
 plus extra to serve
pinch of sea salt
3 cups Greek yogurt

Turkish cotton candy, to serve

A wispy mound of Turkish cotton candy crowns this yogurt. Known as pismaniye or pashmak, it is a spun confection made with flour, butter, sugar, and often sesame or nuts, giving it the taste of a biscotti but with a cloudlike texture that dissolves instantly on the tongue. It is worth seeking out as it is the easiest way to lift a dessert from simple to ethereal.

Prepare the honeyed walnuts in advance: Preheat the oven to 325°F. Toss the nuts with the honey and salt, and spread out on a baking sheet lined with parchment. Bake for 10 minutes, tossing halfway through, until the nuts are glazed and golden. Keep an eye on them, as they'll burn quickly. Let cool.

When you are ready to serve, spoon the yogurt into individual small bowls, top with a sprinkling of the honeyed walnuts, and finally a tangled mound of the Turkish cotton candy. Put the pot of honey on the table for people to drizzle over as they eat.

Ruins of a Russian Count's Castle

Serves 6 to 8

For the meringues

2 large egg whites
  (about ⅓ cup)
⅓ cup superfine sugar
½ cup confectioners' sugar,
  sifted
2 teaspoons cocoa powder,
  sifted

For the cake

½ cup dried prunes, pitted
and
  coarsely chopped
½ cup walnuts, coarsely
  chopped
⅔ cup all-purpose flour
1½ teaspoons baking powder
5 tablespoons soft butter,
  plus extra for greasing
⅓ cup superfine sugar
1 jumbo egg
2 ounces dark chocolate, for
  decorating

For the cream

¾ cup heavy cream
¾ cup sour cream

This magnificently named cake is a Russian creation and very popular for celebrations in Uzbekistan. There are many different versions including meringue, sponge, even profiteroles, but always piled into precarious towers like the crumbling ruins of a hilltop castle.

Start by making the meringues: Preheat the oven to 200°F. Line two baking sheets with parchment paper.

Whisk the egg whites to the soft peak stage and add the superfine sugar, a spoonful at a time, whisking until the mixture is thick, very glossy and very smooth. Fold in the confectioners' sugar, add the cocoa powder, and fold until the brown just ripples through the white. Spoon or pipe meringues about 1½ inches in diameter on the parchment paper. Bake for 1 hour, or until firm and crisp. Cool and store in an airtight container until needed.

To make the cake, preheat the oven to 325°F. Grease and line an 8-inch cake pan.

Start by mixing the prunes and walnuts with a small spoonful of the flour, just to give them a dusty coating. Set aside. Sift the remaining flour and the baking powder into a roomy mixing bowl. Add the butter, sugar, and egg, and use a hand-held mixer to mix for about 1 minute until smooth and creamy. Use a metal spoon to fold the prunes and nuts into the mixture, and spread the mixture into the cake pan. Bake for 25 minutes, or until the cake is springy to the touch. Turn out onto a wire rack and let cool completely.

To make the cream, beat the two creams together until they just form stiff peaks. Spread the top and sides of the cake with some of the cream. Coarsely crumble four or five of the meringues into the remaining cream and fold together. Pile this mixture in a mound on top of the cake. Position the remaining meringues into the cream to cover the surface.

For a final flourish, melt the chocolate in a heatproof bowl over a pan of simmering water. Let cool, then drizzle over the top.

Shopping under Kyrgyzstan's sacred mountain

"The nectarine and curious peach
Into my hands themselves do reach."
Andrew Marvell

Unlike arriving at Samarkand for the first time, overloaded with myth, fantasy, and expectations, I had no idea what to expect from Osh. On first impressions, Kyrgyzstan's second city seems like a throwback to a lost world. In the central park an old Aeroflot plane (today used as a photo booth) lies nose-to-the-ground next to a rusty Ferris wheel and a canvas-sided yurt café. The city is also home to an aging statue of Lenin. It is probably an exaggeration to claim that Osh is older than Rome, but no one really knows who founded this city. Some say it was Alexander the Great, others King Solomon. Either way, the Mongols flattened it in the thirteenth century before it became a major Silk Road hub.

Eager for respite from the sun, I make my way to the partially canopied Jayma Bazaar. Stretching either side of the wavy Ak-Buura (White Camel) river, stalls spill into every available space on a pockmarked carpet of dust. Under one of the makeshift hessian awnings, I barter for a small *shyrdak* (felt rug) and bag myself a handful of sugar-dusted barsook (fried dough balls) and a freshly baked non bread the size of a bicycle wheel. Stepping over piles of purple garlic heads, I watch as goods as various as apples and live ducklings are weighed on huge rusty scales. Mobile phones aside, there are hardly any signs of mechanical or electronic equipment.

Turning a corner, the craggy top of Sulaiman-Too pans into view. I can just make out a string of people no bigger than ants, schlepping up the steps to the mosque at its summit as countless numbers of pilgrims have done for one and a half millennia. This mountain has been a sacred place for Muslims since ancient times; it is where the founder of the Mughal Dynasty spent his youth and where women come to pray for fertility at a cave called Ene-Beshik. It is a formidable landmark and now a World Heritage Site.

Further along, I stop at a particularly abundant fruit and spice stall and scoop up some peaches while filling my bag with Kyrgyzstan's fine pistachios, almonds, walnuts, and some local black pepper and paprika to take home. The peaches are the best I have tasted anywhere. Heavy with juice, they have a deep-pink flesh and a soft but well-defined sweetness. As I prepare to leave, the vendor, a woman wearing a fabulous leopard-print dress, straightens her green floral head scarf, takes my hand, and ushers me around a corner. There, she dusts off a stool and offers me tea, smiling through a set of twinkling gold teeth. With considerable spirit, she slices up a giant watermelon using a terrifying-looking sword, straight out of *The Arabian Nights*, and asks me where I'm from and why I'm here. Shopping in Osh is an experience as well as a transaction and I'm reminded that hospitality is a national cult in Kyrgyzstan. Over the next half hour we share three cups of tea—and the entire melon.

Kyrgyz woman selling spices in Osh market, Kyrgyzstan

Candied Quinces with Chopped Nuts

Serves 8

4 quinces
2¼ cups sugar
1 cinnamon stick, snapped
   in half
1 cup water
juice of 1 lemon

To serve
½ cup nibbed (chopped)
   almonds
½ cup nibbed (chopped)
   pistachios

Part of the rose family and enriched with a sweet narcissus scent, quinces grow wild in the Caucasus and Central Asia where it is believed the fruit originated.

Long roasting turns the quinces' unyielding flesh first to a blushed pink, eventually darkening to a deep ruby red. With the intensified color comes a magical transformation of flavor; the flesh is both deeply perfumed and toffeed. These are perfect served with a spoonful of ice cream or crème fraîche.

Preheat the oven to 325°F.

Peel the quinces then cut each in half lengthwise. Leave the core in but remove any dirt or pockets of seeds. Scatter half the sugar over the bottom of an ovenproof baking dish and lay the quinces on top, cut side down. Tuck in the cinnamon and sprinkle with the remaining sugar. Pour in the water and lemon juice and cover the dish tightly with aluminum foil. Roast in the oven for 3½ to 4 hours, basting the quinces every hour and more frequently toward the end. You want tender fruit and a deep reddish toffee glaze—be careful it doesn't stick and burn in the final stages of cooking. Baste again as they cool to glaze the quinces.

Serve the quince halves at room temperature with a sprinkling of chopped nuts over the top.

Pomegranate and Vodka Sorbet

Serves 4

3 cups fresh pomegranate
 juice
¼ cup good-quality vodka
2 tablespoons Cointreau
2 tablespoons pomegranate
 molasses
2 tablespoons lemon juice
1¼ cups superfine sugar

The hit of vodka keeps this ice soft and scoopable, somewhere between a sorbet and a granita. Choose pomegranate juice from the refrigerated section, not the juice drink, as this has a better flavor and a tartness to balance the sweet.

Mix all the ingredients together and stir well until the sugar completely dissolves. Pour into a freezerproof container and freeze overnight. For a smoother consistency, stir the sorbet well to break up any ice crystals and return to the freezer for a few more hours.

Serve straight from the freezer, perhaps with another shot of vodka alongside.

Sour Cherry and Apple Compote

Serves 4

4 sweet apples, peeled, cored,
 and sliced
¼ cup dried sweetened sour
 cherries
¼ teaspoon ground cinnamon
¼ teaspoon ground cardamom
splash of apple juice or water
lemon juice
sugar

Cardamom is such a lovely pairing for apples and cherries, making a compote that is at once both comforting and familiar, yet exotic. Serve with a bowl of plain yogurt.

Put the apples, cherries, and spices in a pan and pour in a small splash of apple juice or water. Bring to a simmer, then cover with a lid and lower the heat. Poach gently for 20 minutes, or until the cherries have swollen and the apple is soft through.

Add a squeeze of lemon juice and taste the fruit. It should be sweet and sour. Adjust the seasoning, adding sugar or more lemon juice to sweeten or sharpen. Let cool.

Serve chilled or at room temperature.

Licorice Meringues

2 large egg whites
  (about ⅓ cup)
⅓ cup superfine sugar
½ cup confectioners' sugar,
  sifted
½ teaspoon raw licorice
  powder, or to taste
black gel food coloring
  (optional)

Supermarkets in the Russian quarter of Samarkand have piles of gorgeous baby meringues on the sweet counters, as well as towering meringue-covered confections in the cake cabinets. Licorice, which grows wild in Uzbekistan, adds just a faintly spiced and aniseedy note to these mallow-centered meringue kisses. Make sure you buy a good-quality licorice powder, and taste as you add as strength can vary. You can find licorice powder online.

Preheat the oven to 250°F. Line two baking sheets with parchment paper.

Whisk the egg whites to the soft peak stage, then add the superfine sugar, a spoonful at a time, continuing to whisk until the mixture is thick, very glossy, and smooth. You shouldn't feel grains of sugar left if you rub a little of the mixture between your fingertips. Fold in the confectioners' sugar and licorice powder.

For beautiful swirled meringues, use a paint brush to paint three vertical stripes of food coloring gel along the inside of a piping bag fitted with a ½-inch star nozzle. Or, if you prefer not to pipe, dip a skewer in the food coloring and just ripple the black through the mixture. Pipe or spoon the meringues into rounds 1½-inches in diameter on the parchment paper.

Put into the oven and immediately lower the temperature to 200°F. Bake for 1 hour, or until firm, crisp, and easy to lift from the parchment. Cool and store in an airtight container.

Pistachio Halva

Makes about 24 pieces

1¼ cups pistachios
3 cups all-purpose flour
14 tablespoons soft butter
  (1 stick + 6 tablespoons)
¾ cup superfine sugar

Halva, literally meaning sweet, is a word used throughout Central Asia, Eastern Europe, and the Arabic and Jewish worlds. It refers to confections made either with sweetened tahini or with flour and butter. Some are chewy, some have nuts, others melt in your mouth. One of my favorite versions that I had at a chaikana in Uzbekistan uses pistachio flour. It is dense yet crumbly, like a fudgy brownie that requires no baking.

Preheat the oven to 250°F and line a 10 x 12-inch baking sheet with parchment paper.

Unless you're lucky enough to find skinless pistachios (often sold as nibbed in Middle-Eastern shops), you first need to remove the pistachio skins. Soak the nuts in hot water for 10 minutes, then rub off the skins using a clean kitchen towel. Dry the pistachios for about 10 minutes in the oven.

Put the pistachios into a food processor and pulse until coarsely chopped. Remove a handful and set aside, then continue to pulse the rest to a beautiful fine green rubble. (Process too much and you'll end up with pistachio butter.) Mix together the fine and coarsely ground nuts and set aside.

Put the flour in a shallow pan and toast over medium–high heat, stirring all the time, to cook out the raw flavor. Nothing will seem to happen for a while, then the color will begin to change. Be careful the flour doesn't stick and burn. You are after a color somewhere between ivory and pale brown.

Remove the flour from the heat and pour into a bowl. Let cool for 5 minutes, stirring occasionally. Add the butter, sugar, and pistachios, and stir together. Once it is cool enough to handle, you can begin to knead it to make a firm dough.

Press the dough into the lined pan, first with your fingers, then using the back of a spoon to really compress it together. It will seem very crumbly but don't worry; it will firm as it sets. Use a knife to score the halva into diamonds and put the pan into the fridge to chill overnight.

Slice along the score lines before serving. Store in the fridge. It makes a perfect pairing for one of the spiced teas on page 182.

Stuffed Apricots

Makes 10

10 large unsulphered dried apricots
⅓ cup walnuts plus 10 walnut halves
3 tablespoons black raisins
1 tablespoon honey

Energy balls made from raisins and walnuts are given to pregnant women in many parts of Central Asia, and carried by climbers in the High Pamirs. Stuffing this mixture into a dried apricot makes for a sweet and incredibly healthy snack. Make sure you choose unsulphered apricots.

Make a small cut at one end of each apricot and use the handle of a teaspoon to form a cavity. If they are too dry to do this, soften the fruit first by soaking for 10 minutes in warm water.

Pound the walnuts to a fine rubble using a mortar and pestle, then mix in the raisins and honey.

Stuff the raisin mixture into the apricots and plug the openings with a walnut half.

Sesame, Almond, and Ginger Brittle

Makes about 25 to 30 pieces

1 cup sugar

¼ cup honey

¾ cup sesame seeds

¾ cup whole blanched almonds

2 tablespoons butter

2½ ounces candied ginger, coarsely chopped

1 scant teaspoon baking soda

Sesame brittle is a popular sweet in Uzbekistan, and this version with almonds and ginger is so addictive. Baking soda aerates and lightens the caramel, while candied ginger gives a little chew alongside the snap.

Line a baking sheet with baking parchment.

Put the sugar, honey, and ⅓ cup of water into a pan and cook gently without stirring until the sugar melts. Turn the heat up to high and add the sesame seeds and almonds. Cook, stirring almost continuously, as the sugar first bubbles then begins to caramelize and darken. Continue stirring until the seeds and sugar are a rich caramel color, then remove from the heat.

Mix in the butter and, once it has melted and been fully incorporated, the candied ginger, then the baking soda, which will make the mixture foam a little. Pour onto the pan and use the back of a spoon to smooth it out to about ¾-inch thick. It will make a rectangle roughly 8 x 11 inches. Let cool completely.

Turn onto a cutting board and cut into squares. Store in an airtight container. It will last for ages but does get a little sticky with time.

Plum and Raisin Leather

Makes about 10 pieces
(recipe easily doubles)

6 fresh plums, halved, pitted,
   and chopped
⅔ cup raisins
juice of ½ lemon
sugar

From stalls on Azeri roadsides, rounds of fruit leathers hang, glistening like stained glass in the sunshine. Mulberry, apricot, plum, and peach leathers are all popular because these fruit grow in abundance in these parts. Sour plum leather is used to add a tart note to cooking, while this sweet version makes the perfect snack.

Line one or two small baking sheets with parchment paper.

Put the plums and raisins in a pan with ⅓ cup of water and lemon juice. Bring to a simmer, cover, and cook until the plums are collapsed and tender. Transfer to a blender and process until very smooth. Return to the pan and cook gently to thicken the purée.

Remove from the heat and check for sweetness, stirring in sugar to taste if you think it needs it.

Spread the purée over the baking sheet in a thin and even layer, about ¼-inch thick. Put it into the oven and turn to 140°F. Cook for 6 to 8 hours, until the leather is no longer sticky and easy to pull away from the parchment. Let cool completely before rolling the leather, with its parchment, and cutting into individual pieces using scissors or a sharp knife.

Index

Acknowledgments

Firstly, *katta rakhmat* to the people of Central Asia and the Caucasus who have shamed me with their kindness and hospitality over the years.

Closer to home, a big thanks to Heather Holden-Brown for helping the idea along and cutting the deals. Many thanks must also go to the photographers I have admired and worked with over the years who have supplied some great shots for this book, including Matthieu Paley, Christoper Herwig, Richard Haughton, and Theodore Kaye. Thanks also to Bijan Omrani and Hugh Philpott for their time and input, and to Magnus Bartlett and Lucy Kelaart who both inspired my first trip to Central Asia.

Most of all thanks to James for reading, advising and for being patient with me.

CAROLINE

During my time in Samarkand, I was overwhelmed by the generosity of cooks who allowed me into their kitchens and bakeries to share their culinary secrets. I would also like to thank the following people at home who have been invaluable with their recipe testing, insight, or support in this project: Kirsty Smallwood, Amanda Nicholas, Kate Ford, Pip Rau, Lesley Morley, Roopa Gulati. Most of all, thank you to Otto, who happily became a plov enthusiast aged one, and to Sebastian for his unfailing support.

ELEANOR

We would both like to thank the Samarkand team for their heroic patience and hard work. Kyle Cathie, Sophie Allen, Laura Edwards, Patrick Budge, Linda Tubby, Tabitha Hawkins, Hannah Coughlin, and Stephanie Evans—we couldn't have done it without you. And, last but not least, a big thank you to Omar Masom of London's fabulous Turkmen Gallery for loaning us some spectacular props.

Photographic Acknowledgments

All photography by Laura Edwards except pages:
6: top—Christopher Herwig; bottom—Doug Meikle, Dreaming Track Image/ Getty Images. 9: top—Christopher Herwig; bottom—Lois Davilla/ Getty Images. 10-11: top left, bottom middle and bottom right—Christopher Herwig; bottom left—Michal Korta; top right—Caroline Eden. 12: Stephane Godin/Getty Images. 14-15: Christopher Herwig. 17: top—DDP, Camera Press London; bottom—Christopher Herwig. 19: Hans Van Rhoon/Camera Press London. 20-21: top left—Christopher Herwig; top right—Michal Korta; bottom right—James Strachen/Getty Images; bottom middle—Caroline Eden; bottom left—Matthieu Paley. 30: imageBROKER/Alamy. 44: Travel Ink/Getty Images. 56: top—Jean-Philippe Tournut /Getty Images; bottom—Matthieu Paley. 58: top—Caroline Eden; bottom—Matthieu Paley/ National Geographic Creative/Bridgeman Images. 66: top—James Strachan/Getty Images; bottom—Christopher Herwig. 72: top—Leisa Tyler/Getty Images; bottom—Ian Trower/Getty Images. 96, 98, 99: Richard Haughton. 108: top—Jane Sweeney/JAI/Corbis; bottom—DDP, Camera Press London. 114: top—Christopher Herwig; bottom—Matthieu Paley. 142: Matthieu Paley. 148: 'Soviet Stars', from the book *Russian Textiles* © Susan Mellor. 150: AGF/Universal Images Group/Bridgeman Images. 154: top—Magdalena Paluchowska/Alamy; bottom—Stephen Frink Collection/Alamy. 162: Caroline Eden. 164-165: Christopher Herwig. 178: Michal Korta. 184: top—Kasia Nowak/Alamy; bottom—Theodore Kaye. 206: Mariusz Prusaczyk/Alamy.